SECRETARY'S
COMPLETE
Model Letter HANDBOOK

SECRETARY'S
COMPLETE

Model Letter HANDBOOK

Claire Neff Eddings

RENTICE-HALL, INC., ENGLEWOOD CLIFFS, N.J.

Twenty-Fourth Printing . . . . . March, 1979

79740—B & P

HOW THIS BOOK
WILL HELP YOU

The sample letters contained within this book are just that—*samples*. They can be used —copied, if you will—virtually intact for many correspondence situations by simply changing names, dates or figures which appear.

Sometimes the phrasing of one letter can be combined with some of the phrasing from another letter to fit a given circumstance. Basic letters can be reworded, revised and adapted to fit most of the letter-writing situations which confront the secretary.

While there are many hundreds of letters in this book, the secretary may, of course, not find every letter she looks for within its pages. However, the language and style of many of the letters herein will surely suggest a way to handle a particular situation.

Chapter headings categorize the type of letter in each chapter. Sub-headings, further categorizing every *pair* of letters in every chapter, and indicating the specific approach, will prove most helpful. To further speed up the secretary's search for the proper letter, a complete index appears in the back of the book.

Contents

I

Letters WRITTEN OVER

THE SECRETARY'S SIGNATURE

❦ There are some business letters that always go out of the office over the secretary's signature. These are the letters written by the secretary during her employer's absence. They are, primarily, letters written by the secretary to delay action until the employer's return. This is not only a courteous practice but essential to the maintenance of a company's image in the areas of promptness and public relations. A qualified secretary gives the practice a topmost place in her secretarial job functions.

These delayed action letters fall into two categories: (1) straight acknowledgment, (2) acknowledgment with a direct answer.

CHECK LIST
FOR LETTERS OVER THE SECRETARY'S SIGNATURE

1. Explain the reason why you are writing instead of your employer.

2. Don't make any commitments unless you are so authorized.

3. Be gracious and willing to help.

Incoming letter

Dear Mr. Little,

I'm ready to talk—about the real estate project we've been plotting. The blueprints are drawn. The price list is complete. I have the names of the architects and builders who will bid on the deal.

Can we have lunch sometime soon? Perhaps May 2nd or 3rd?

Very truly yours,

Answering letter

Secretary Changes Appointment

Dear Mr. Berry,

Mr. Little is in Los Angeles and is not expected back in the office until May 3rd. However, before he left, he indicated he was anxious to get together with you shortly after his return.

Will you telephone me here at Murray Hill 2-1400 and et me know if lunch on Tuesday, May 7th, is convenient? If so, I'll make this a definite appointment for you and Mr. Little.

Very truly yours,

Incoming letter

Dear Mr. Small,

The MAGIC Sealer is now in full production at our plant—and I am most anxious to demonstrate this fine new product to you. I believe it will speed up your canning operation by more than 25 percent.

Will you let me know when it will be convenient for me to call on you, Mr. Small? I'm ready with a written proposal for either leasing or purchase.

Cordially,

Answering letter

Delaying Appointment Indefinitely

Dear Mr. Manning,

Mr. Small is in Los Angeles at the moment. Before he left, however, he indicated that little could be accomplished at this time at any meeting in connection with your proposal. He has asked me to write, when I heard from you, suggesting that the matter be tabled for several months. He hopes you will contact him again in the early fall, at which time perhaps the opportunity for demonstration and consideration will be more favorable.

Very truly yours,

Incoming letter

Dear Mr. Little,

At long last, I'm ready to discuss the program you had in mind when last we met. I have some worthwhile ideas, I think, but naturally would like to confirm our financial arrangements before we go into further detail.

I'd appreciate a note from you at your early convenience, putting into writing your verbally-stated proposition to place me on a retainer basis at $500 a month starting July 1st. At the same time, perhaps you'll want to name the most convenient day for us to get together.

Cordially,

Answering letter

Confirming Verbal Agreement

Dear Mr. Berry,

Mr. Little is in Los Angeles and not expected back in the office until June 15th. However, before he left, he authorized me to tell you that the $500 retainer can go into effect when you are ready to become active with the program you discussed. Therefore, this will confirm the arrangement and your first check will be issued on July 1st and mailed to your home.

If you'll phone me on June 18th, I'll be happy to set up a lunch date for you and Mr. Little at a mutually convenient time and place.

Very truly yours,

Incoming letter

Dear Mrs. Black,

Happily enough, the package you sent me arrived this morning just as I planned to sit down and write you a nasty letter of complaint, my second such! Instead, this is just to let you know that the package was postmarked on the date you promised to mail it. The delay was definitely at the post office level and I apologize for my lack of faith in your prompt service.

Not incidentally, I'm extremely pleased with the contents of the package. It's nice to know that your Personal Shopper has such excellent taste that customers can depend on her judgment.

Cordially,

Answering letter

To a Satisfied Customer

Dear Miss Hopewell,

We don't like to blame Uncle Sam for everything, but I'm certainly glad that the Post Office Department was responsible for the delayed arrival of your package. Much as I hate to admit it, we're not perfect and there was always the chance that somewhere along the line someone had "goofed" in the shipment of your purchases.

I've passed along your compliments to Miss Dugan, our Personal Shopper, who was happy to hear such nice words of praise.

Thanks so much for writing us.

Cordially,

Incoming letter

Dear Mr. Pieper,

Can you supply me with facts and figures which will help me to prepare a 15-minute talk, to be given at the

Architectural Engineering Society's annual convention late this month, in connection with urban renewal in the city of Hartford?

I understand you chaired the board which financed the 10-year plan. Can you tell me how you arrived at the figure you recommended for expenditure over the 10-year period? Also, how did you decide which projects were of foremost importance? Is there a specific annual budget for the entire 10-year period, to be spent at only a certain rate annually, or can you utilize the 10-year fund in any fashion you see fit provided that the end-result accomplishes your aim?

I shall most certainly appreciate any information and help you can give me.

Cordially,

Answering letter

Supplying Information

Dear Mr. Crane,

Mr. Pieper has asked me to answer your recent letter and I think the enclosed proposal sheets will give you the information you want.

These sheets show the initial proposal for a 10-year plan, and a breakdown of the suggested yearly segments of the plan. Since Mr. Pieper and the board felt that the most urgent requirement was to provide adequate parking space in the area concerned with renewal, you will note that the first year's financing is for twice the amount indicated for the nine subsequent years.

Since each detail is well spelled out in the proposal, I'm sure no additional explanation is necessary. However, please feel free to call me if I can be of any further help.

Cordially,

Incoming letter

Dear Mr. Bunting,

Our books show that the bill for the installation of air conditioning in your office on South Street has not been paid in full. There is an outstanding amount of $150.00.

Will you kindly check your records and let us know right away if this amount has been paid? If not, we would appreciate payment at your early convenience.

Thank you very much.

Cordially,

Answering letter

Checking Records

Dear Sirs,

Our records show that a check for $150 was mailed to you on December 20th, 1964 and it was not returned with our December or January bank statement.

Mr. Bunting has asked me to stop payment of this check and another will be issued at once. Thank you for calling this to our attention.

Cordially,

Incoming letter

Dear Mr. Baxter,

About six weeks ago I wrote asking you to plan an itinerary for a trip through the Scandinavian countries for the spring of 1967.

To date, I have not heard from you, and I am wondering if you failed to receive my letter.

Will you let me know right away if you received my letter? If not, I can send you a copy of the tentative schedule as I had planned it.

Cordially,

Answering letter

Explaining Delay

Dear Mrs. Harkness,

Mr. Baxter did receive your letter of November 18th, and there was some delay in getting started on your itinerary, because of the rush for holiday cruises.

I'm glad to tell you however, that Mr. Baxter is now working on your itinerary and it will be in the mail at the end of this week.

He is very sorry about the delay and hopes you have not been inconvenienced by it.

Cordially,

Incoming letter

Dear Sirs,

The 1964 real estate tax on the property in the name of Emily Bogart, now deceased, remains unpaid. The 1963 tax was paid by an interested party, who does not wish to pay it this year.

As Trustees for this estate, I am wondering if you have any suggestions about this property and the overdue taxes.

Will you kindly write me at your early convenience?

Cordially,

Answering letter

Supplying Information

Dear Mrs. Sleeper,

Your recent letter relative to the Emily Bogart property has been received by Mr. Hanson.

For a number of years, taxes were paid on the property by the Masonic Homes with the hope that the lot would have some value. Many attempts were made to sell it, but no offer of any kind was forthcoming.

After worrying with the property for nearly five years, it was decided that the property would be abandoned. Mr. Hanson suggests, therefore, that the interested party to whom you refer is free to take such action as desired.

Very truly yours,

Incoming letter

Dear Mr. Abercrombie,

We have received our real estate tax bill for the year 1964 on our property in Goldensville. Will you please note in your records that the icehouse was torn down this spring so that we won't be taxed for it next year?

Thank you very much.

Very truly yours,

Answering letter

Acknowledging Information

Dear Mrs. Finch,

The information about your icehouse being torn down has been passed along to the Chairman of the Board of Assessors, Mr. Abercrombie. I have also made a note of this on your records and the tax for next year will be adjusted accordingly when the Board sets the rate for 1965.

Cordially,

II

Letters OF ACKNOWLEDGMENT

❦ Today, most companies have a standard acknowledgment form which is sent almost automatically on such routine matters as the receipt of a contract, an order, or a check. From time to time, however, a special situation arises which requires personal handling. One of the basic rules for composing such letters is that, whenever possible, the customer should be *thanked* for whatever is being acknowledged —whether it be a letter, a suggestion, a package, or even a complaint.

CHECK LIST
FOR LETTERS OF ACKNOWLEDGMENT

1. Write as promptly as possible.
2. Spell out what has been received.
3. Thank the person to whom you are writing.

Incoming letter

Dear Mrs. Chase,

    This is just a reminder to let you know that we have you scheduled to speak at our Kiwanis luncheon on August 3rd. The luncheon starts at 12:00 noon and we are certainly looking forward to having you with us and to listening to one of your very fine speeches on "Travel in the Congo."

                                        Cordially,

Answering letter

Speaking Engagement

Dear Mr. Johnstone,

    Your letter reminding Mrs. Chase of her appointment to speak at the Kiwanis luncheon on August 3rd has arrived while Mrs. Chase is away from the office. However, she considers that date a definite one and has made plans to leave here that morning in time to arrive at the luncheon no later than 11:45 A.M. She will appreciate your kind reminder, I am sure.

                                        Cordially,

Incoming letter

Dear Mr. Davis,

    Under separate cover I am sending you an advance copy of my latest book, *Making Ends Meet in Business*. I hope you'll find time to read it soon and I would appreciate your comments.

Cordially,

Answering letter

A Book

Dear Mr. Hull,

This will acknowledge receipt this morning of your book, *Making Ends Meet in Business*, which you so kindly sent to Mr. Davis. He's been looking forward to reading this book, I know, having seen the favorable reviews in various trade magazines. Upon his return to the office next Monday, I know he'll drop you a personal note of thanks. Meantime, I wanted you to know that the book arrived and is being held for him.

Cordially,

Incoming letter

Dear Mr. Jones,

In order to get under way with the survey you have asked us to do for your Planning Board, we will need the following information:
1. Number of acres in proposed zoning area
2. Proposed division of acreage
3. Number of houses already existing in area

Will you kindly let us know by return mail an ap proximate date when you can have this material ready for us, so that we can start the survey without further delay?

Cordially,

Answering letter

Request for Information

Dear Mr. Thomas,

This will acknowledge receipt of your letter of May 10th, addressed to Mr. Jones, in connection with the survey you are about to undertake for our Planning Board. Mr. Jones is out of town until Friday, but I want to assure you that your letter will be given his immediate attention when he returns. If there are any questions, he will call you promptly.

Very truly yours,

Incoming letter

Dear Mr. Little,

When we last met for luncheon on May 15th, I understood that we would have another meeting at the end of June to go over the contracts for the new Regional School building. Please let me know right away if you will be free for another luncheon meeting—perhaps June 28th, at 12:00 noon, and at the Town House Grill?

Cordially,

Answering letter

An Appointment

Dear Mr. Berry,

Mr. Little is out of town until June 15th. Upon his return, I am sure he will contact you at once, since I know he is anxious to follow through on his tentative arrangement with you. You may be sure I'll call your letter to his attention.

Cordially,

Incoming letter

Dear Mr. Little,

Recently you ordered two of our "SCAT" outboard motors Model No. A, to be shipped to your camp. This particular model has been discontinued and superseded by Model A2. We think the improvements made in Model A2 will make it an even more serviceable purchase, as you will see from the enclosed descriptive literature.

Will you please let us know at once, Mr. Little, if we should fill your order with the "SCAT" A2?

Cordially,

Answering letter

A Change in Order

Dear Mr. Berry,

Because Mr. Little is out of town until June 15th, I'm acknowledging your letter of June 8th. He will give it his immediate attention upon his return and you can expect to hear from him shortly after that.

Cordially,

Incoming letter

Dear Mr. Black,

After you left the Miramar Hotel yesterday afternoon, the maid found an electric razor in the bathroom; because your initials were on the cover, we knew that it must belong to you. We're sending it on its way to you in this evening's mail, insured.

We hope we will have the pleasure of seeing you soon again, Mr. Black.

Cordially,

Answering letter

Forgotten Articles

Dear Mr. Stevens,

This will acknowledge receipt of the package you forwarded to Mr. Black. I know he'll be happy to have his razor once again and I'll see that he gets it immediately upon his return to the office on Thursday.

Very truly yours,

III

Letters DELAYING ACTION

❧ Of course, it is not only the secretary who writes letters attempting to delay action. Frequently also, her employer will write such letters on his own—or ask for help in drafting them for his signature.

It's helpful to remember when putting together such letters that there must always be a good reason behind the need for such delay. The pace of modern business is fast, indeed, and a weak or unbelievable reason for slowing up any phase of a business project will lead to bad will, loss of potential business, or even a reputation for procrastination.

Study the letters which follow. In each instance, a plausible excuse is offered for any unavoidable delay. In some cases, the reason is offered in such a fashion that it will earn the sympathy of the recipient.

CHECK LIST
FOR LETTERS DELAYING ACTION

1. Apologize for the delay.
2. Explain the delay.
3. Offer a substitute and more prompt service where possible.
4. Promise to expedite.

Incoming letter

Dear Mr. Worth,

Under separate cover I'm forwarding to you a copy of the complete report about fluoridation. This report, as you know, was put together on a confidential basis by two laboratory technicians at Baltimore who became interested in the subject well beyond the limits of the technical experiments they were hired to perform.

I know you will respect the confidence in which this report is sent to you for your perusal, and I'd appreciate it very much if you will return it to me, at my home, as quickly as possible.

Cordially,

Answering letter

Out of Town

Dear Dr. Castle,

Your letter of May 10th to Mr. Worth and the report you sent under separate cover arrived this morning. Mr. Worth is out of town at the moment, but I know he'll be extremely appreciative of your kindness in sending him this confidential material.

I'm sure you'll hear from Mr. Worth immediately upon

his return to the office. Meantime, I have put your letter and the report into his confidential file and shall bring them to his immediate attention.

Cordially,

Incoming letter

Dear Mr. Rachel,

Is it possible for us to get together sometime within the next week? I need some facts and figures about the railroad industry and I know you have put together some valuable material.

I need this information by the 10th of this month, since the statistics will be included in a report I shall make to the State Transportation Board on January 13th. So I'd appreciate an immediate answer from you setting up an appointment as soon as possible.

May I hear from you by return mail, please?

Cordially,

Answering letter

Out of Town—Secretary Offers Assistance

Dear Mr. Madden,

Your letter to Mr. Rachel arrived in this morning's mail and I'm sorry to say that Mr. Rachel is out of town until the 15th.

I realize that his return will be too late for him to gather together the material you need for your report to the State Transportation Board. Perhaps I can put together some of these statistics for you, since I have access to Mr. Rachel's files.

If you wish me to do this, I'll need to discuss the matter with you in person and very quickly. Will you call me to arrange for an hour or two here, if you feel my efforts can serve the purpose? I'll be happy to do what I can.

Cordially,

Incoming letter

Dear Mr. Madden,

I am writing to ask if it will still be convenient for you to go over the deed on Jones's property at the meeting we had scheduled for July 12th.

If it is not possible for you to be in the New York office on that day, will you kindly let me know at once?

Cordially,

Answering letter

Cancelling Appointment—Out of Town

Dear Mrs. Dean,

I regret very much that Mr. Madden will be unable to keep his appointment with you on July 12th, as previously scheduled. An emergency in our Chicago office has made it necessary for him to fly out there and he will not be back in New York until July 14th.

If you wish to arrange for another appointment, just drop me a line and let me know. The calendar looks reasonably clear for the week of July 21st.

Cordially,

Incoming letter

Dear Mr. Jones,

My associates and I will hold our monthly luncheon meeting in our offices on Friday, August 10th, at 1:00 P.M., and I am most anxious to have you present at that time to discuss the union matter with them.

Will you please let me know by return mail if you can make it?

Cordially,

Answering letter

Cancelling Appointment—Illness

Dear Mr. Mooney,

The prospect of visiting with you at your office on August 10th and meeting your associates was a very pleasing one to Mr. Jones and he had looked forward to the date with great interest. That's why I'm extremely sorry to tell you that he will be unable to keep the appointment, due to the illness of his wife.

At present, we just don't know when Mr. Jones will be back at his desk, but I'll be happy to notify you as soon as he is, with the thought that perhaps another appointment can be arranged at your convenience.

Cordially,

Incoming letter

Dear Mr. Dunham,

I am looking forward to our meeting in Genoa, on June 15th, with great pleasure.

The reservations for two single rooms with bath at the Excelsior were confirmed by air yesterday. I'll be waiting for your call just as soon as you arrive there after your trip from Rome.

Cordially,

Answering letter

Cancelling Appointment—Illness

Dear Mr. Deming,

I know you will be sorry to learn that Mr. Dunham's trip to Italy has been postponed and he will be unable to meet with you at Genoa, as previously arranged.

The postponement is due to the serious illness of his father, and, since the senior Mr. Dunham is not expected to live, I'm sure you will understand why Mr. Dunham, Jr. cannot leave the country at this time.

Mr. Dunham will no doubt write to you as soon as possible and has asked me to tell you that he is terribly sorry that he will be unable to join you.

Cordially,

Incoming letter

Dear Uncle Jim,

This is to let you know that I am still planning to arrive in New York on July 22nd as I wired you last week when I received your letter about the job opening in the clerical department.

Since two weeks have passed, I'm wondering if the position is still open. Will you let me know right away, please? As much as I would love to see you and have a nice long visit with you, I do feel that I should wait until something else turns up—that is, if I've missed this chance.

Sally and Henrietta join me in sending much love to you,

Your favorite niece!

Answering letter

Position Filled

My dear Martha,

The opening in our clerical department has been filled, and I am sorry to have to tell you that there is no other opportunity available here at this time.

This means that there is not much use in your coming to New York on Monday, July 22nd, as you had planned. You can rest assured that I will keep my eyes wide open for anything else that may come up since I am so anxious to see you in the job niche which suits your personality and ability, to say nothing of how much fun it will be to have my favorite niece living nearby in New York City. You'll be hearing from me very soon, I'm sure.

Your affectionate uncle,

Incoming letter

Dear Miss Mannix,

On Thursday, December 14th, the Chorale Society will meet for luncheon at the Plaza to honor its retiring chairman, Mr. Daniel Thompson. As you know, Mr. Thompson has served without salary for seven years and has brought to successful fruition every single one of the goals set up when the Society was formed.

As a long-time friend and associate of Mr. Thompson's,

we hope you can attend the luncheon and wonder if you would be kind enough to sit on the dais. Also, it would be most appreciated and fitting if you will speak for about five minutes, giving the background story of the founding of the Chorale Society, a story you know so well.

Will you please drop me a line at your earliest convenience, letting me know if your schedule will permit you to be with us?

Cordially,

Answering letter

Out of Town—Delay Acceptance

Dear Mr. Bender,

Miss Mannix is on a business trip to Detroit and your letter arrived the day after she left.

However, I've checked her schedule and find that her present plans for December 14th would make it impossible for her to attend the Chorale Society luncheon in honor of Mr. Daniel Thompson on that day.

I shall call your letter to her attention immediately upon her return to the office, for it may be possible for her to switch a date or two in order to accept your kind invitation. You will hear from her early next week.

Cordially,

Incoming letter

Dear Miss Skinner,

Mr. Thomasino is so lucky to have a secretary as capable as you are. You've always been so helpful and I wonder if I can call on you for another favor.

I'm anxious to get together with Mr. Thomasino as soon as possible to show him a film made at our main plant, which explains the process by which we coat tape.

Could I prevail upon you to set aside an hour for me some morning next week? Once Mr. Thomasino understands the tape-coating process, I'm sure he'll see its advantages and give me an initial order.

Anything you can do to arrange for this appointment will be most appreciated. I'll wait to hear from you.

Cordially,

Answering letter

Out of Town—No Authority to Make Appointment

Dear Mr. Hull,

I wish I could do as you ask, but I cannot make an appointment for Mr. Thomasino without his consent. In addition, he will be out of town all next week.

I'd suggest that you contact Mr. Thomasino by phone the week after next. Then, if he wishes to set aside time to see the film you mention, I'm sure he will tell you when it would be most convenient.

Cordially,

Incoming letter

Dear Mrs. Budd,

Our new product, the General Polisher and Scrubber, is now ready for demonstration, and it seems only natural that I should look forward to coming over to your inn at an early date, to show you how helpful it would be to you and your staff.

With less effort than vacuuming your rugs, it will give your floors the softly glowing satin finish that you need to complement your fine furnishings. It glides over the floors, close into corners, right up to baseboards and under furniture.

I would like to show you the General in operation soon, as I know you are always interested in the newest labor-saving devices. Will you be at the inn on Thursday about 2:00 P.M.? I will plan to stop in at that time.

Cordially,

Answering letter

Not Ready for Demonstration

Dear Mr. Nealy,

Mrs. Budd has asked me to write in answer to your recent letter. At this particular time, we are simply not in the market for a new floor polisher so it would not be advantageous for you to stop by on Thursday.

Perhaps at some future date you will want to write me again, in case circumstances change. Thanks so much, nevertheless, for letting us know about this new machine.

Cordially,

Incoming letter

Dear Mrs. Rogers,

There are several reasons why I believe it would be to the advantage of Doane, Inc., to give me an early opportunity to demonstrate our new legal-size portable typewriters. These machines are built on a new principle developed less than a year ago by the Swiss. They weigh about half what an ordinary electric portable weighs, and this in spite of the fact that there is an oversize carriage as part of the standard equipment.

I'd like you to see this machine in action, have some of your typists try it, and then listen to the amazingly low price I can offer you.

I'll be in your area next Tuesday right after the lunch hour. I will stop in at that time with the hope that you can spare me about 15 minutes.

Cordially,

Answering letter

Illness—Refer to Assistant

Dear Mr. Crandall,

Mrs. Rogers is at home this week, laid low by a mild but annoying case of the flu. In any case, she would simply refer you to Mr. Jason Amrill, our office manager, who is in charge of purchasing.

When you're in the neighborhood next Tuesday, why not stop in and ask for Mr. Amrill? I'll alert him to the possibility that you will want to see him and if there is any reason why he will not be available, I'll have him drop you a line.

Cordially,

IV

Letters OF APOLOGY

❦ While sound business practice calls for immediate or nearly immediate treatment of most matters, the human element sometimes intrudes and causes an unanticipated delay. Occasionally, a letter which requires a prompt reply will become lost in the shuffle and found later. Sick leave or vacations can cut down on office efficiency temporarily, also causing undue delay in answering correspondence.

Sometimes, a delay is caused by the need to put together materials to be incorporated in the answer to a letter or a request. At other times, the press of business simply slows up the pace of a correspondent to the point where he is "behind" on all correspondence.

Also, errors in business do occur, much as we try to avoid them. Frank acknowledgement in a letter of apology can be helpful, too. Any offer which makes amends or undoes some of the damage caused by the error will alleviate, to some degree, the annoyance felt by a customer or client.

CHECK LIST

FOR LETTERS OF APOLOGY

1. Apologize with sincerity and regret.
2. Make amends, where possible.
3. Promise to avoid a recurrence.
4. Say "thank you" for tolerance and understanding of the situation.

Incoming letter

Dear Dr. Underwood,

Last spring, when I applied for the term insurance policy now in force with your company, it was necessary that I have a complete physical examination. You completed the examination sometime in early April, as I recall.

Now, my personal physician Dr. Alfred Foote would like very much to make a comparison between the electro-cardiogram findings of that date with the findings of a cardiogram just performed.

Will you be kind enough to forward at once to Dr. Foote a report of your findings last April? His address is 1112 Graham Avenue, Morristown, New Jersey. I shall very much appreciate your cooperation.

Cordially,

Answering letter

Illness—Refer Request to Another

Dear Mr. Watson,

I hope you will forgive the extreme delay in answering your letter of the 9th. Dr. Underwood has been seriously ill since the middle of January and it has taken me some time to locate the records you referred to.

Fortunately, they're now in my hands and I have asked Dr. Jonas Miller, another of our examiners, to prepare a report from them so that it can be forwarded to Dr. Foote.

I hope that the report will be completed this week, so it should be in Dr. Foote's hands no later than the 20th of this month.

Thank you so much for your patience.

Cordially,

Incoming letter

Dear Mr. Carlson,

It has been three weeks since you were here to see us and to discuss the proposed contract for the new factory building.

We do not want to seem to rush you—but there is the matter of scheduling the work load both here in the office and at the site, so we are anxious to know if you have come to any decision.

Some of your key men may be on vacation, as is the case here, and we can understand the delay. However, I hope you can get some word to us in the very near future.

Kindest regards and best wishes.

Cordially,

Answering letter

General Delay

Dear Mr. Barrette,

Please pardon my tardiness in thanking you for the time and many courtesies you extended during my visit of the 1st.

Not only was the trip a delightful one, but I think that our discussion concerning the proposed contract was very useful.

We are at this moment putting together a proposal for your consideration, including a complete suggested timetable and cost breakdown.

I'll try to get back to you with this within the next week. Once again, thanks for a delightful day.

Cordially,

Incoming letter

Out of Town

Dear Park,

It was a great disappointment to learn that you had been in Boston last week while I was at a convention at White Sulphur Springs. Wouldn't that just be my luck, when we haven't had a visit together for so long?

Well . . . we can't change things now, so this letter is being written not only to tell you how sorry I am that I missed you, but also to find out when you think you might get up this way again.

Why not try for the weekend following Thanksgiving? If that sounds feasible, just let me know and I'll make reservations at your favorite spot.

Cordially,

Answering letter

Dear Mal,

There were some special problems which I wanted to discuss with you when I was in Boston last week. Now, fortunately, it won't be too long before I will see you because I am delighted to say that I can accept your kind invitation for the weekend following Thanksgiving.

Please reserve a suite for me at the Palace, for three days. I will arrive Friday at 9:00 A.M. If you would like to have

Paul sit in with us for this meeting, I'd like it very much, but I'll leave that to your discretion. I'll call you on my arrival.

Cordially,

Incoming letter

Dear Mrs. Stern,

You're prompt enough about collecting premiums when they're due. But you're apparently not quite so anxious to make refunds when that becomes necessary.

Two months ago, as you know, I changed my residence and instructed you to reduce the amount of homeowner's insurance I carried, since my new home is of less value than the previous one.

You wrote me at that time that, because of this reduction, there would be a rebate in the amount of my premium, which had already been paid on the old house. To date, I'm still waiting for your check. Fifty dollars may not seem like a lot to you, but it's a tidy sum where I'm concerned, and I want my money!

Cordially,

Answering letter

General Delay

Dear Mr. Scofield,

I'm sorry you've had to wait so long for the refund due you, but I'm happy to say that I've just been notified by our accounting department that a check will be mailed to you tomorrow.

Incidentally, the check is for $31.57, not for $50, as you indicated in your letter. Rates have increased since you took out your original policy, but, as you will see if you study the attached brochure, important additional coverage has been added.

Thank you very much for your patience in this matter.

Cordially,

Incoming letter

Dear Mr. Gunner,

I need a complete statement of my stock transactions for the year 1962 and since all of my dealings were through Merriwether, I'd appreciate it very much if you'll put together such a statement right away.

The tabulation should include the number of shares purchased in each transaction, the name of the stock, the date of purchase, and the price per share. It should also include brokerage costs on each transaction. If the stock was subsequently sold, I need a similar breakdown in connection with its sale. It will also be necessary that you give me a record in detail of any sales made for me during 1962 of stock purchased in other years. Where this occurred, I will need a date of purchase and purchase price, plus brokerage fee involved, too.

I realize that this is an annoying assignment since 1962 is well behind us at this time. But Uncle Sam says he wants me to supply this information and he wants to see me, with it in hand, on October 4th. That means I need your detailed report no later than October 3rd.

Your prompt cooperation will certainly be much appreciated.

Cordially,

Answering letter

Out of Office—Refer to Another

Dear Mr. Brown,

Your request for a complete statement of your stock transactions for the year 1962 has been passed along to Mr.

Julius Hatfield who is in charge of this department while Mr. Gunner is away until September 30th.

Mr. Hatfield is familiar with the files and is aware of the urgency of your request. He asked me to let you know that the necessary information will be in your hands well before October 3rd.

Cordially,

Incoming letter

Dear Mr. Tessel,

Before spring arrives and the bug situation gets out of control, we want to plan our spraying schedule for the northern part of the county.

When I saw you some time ago, you told me that you had the tree spraying report from which we could work out our routine spraying schedule. At your earliest convenience, would you be kind enough to send me a copy of this report, please?

With kindest regards, I am,

Cordially,

Answering letter

Out of Town—Illness

Dear Mr. Thompson,

Please excuse the delay in answering your letter of the 7th. Mr. Tessel is out of town and will not return until September 30th. In his absence, I unfortunately was hit with the very prevalent flu "bug" and just got back to my desk this morning.

I believe I can prepare the tree spraying report you need and shall start working on it at once. Unless I run into unanticipated problems, I shall have it in your hands no later than the end of next week.

Cordially,

Incoming letter

Dear Bob,

Many weeks ago, you promised you'd send me a detailed report about the meeting you attended in Los Angeles during the Photographers Convention there. As you know, I need this report to incorporate into the proposed by-laws for our newly formed retailers' organization.

Will you please do your best to get this material to me within the next week?

Cordially,

Answering letter

Out of Town

Dear Jim,

My sincere apologies! I had certainly hoped to get the minutes of our meeting into written form before this and send you a copy. However, I was called to New York immediately after my return from Los Angeles and when I returned last Thursday there were seemingly a dozen things that needed my immediate attention.

I'm putting the minutes together now and hope to have a written draft in shape for you no later than next Tuesday.

Once again, *please* excuse the delay. It was unavoidable.

Cordially,

Incoming letter

Dear Mrs. Whitestone,

Two weeks ago, I wrote you asking for a photostatic copy of a deed which I registered at the courthouse on July 25, 1961. I enclosed with my letter the usual $1 fee for this photostat, and I explained that I needed this copy no later than August 1st.

To date, I have not received the photostat nor any word from you. Will you please write me at once if there is any reason why this photostat is not available? The matter is urgent!

Very truly yours,

Answering letter

Equipment Out of Order

Dear Mr. Prior,

When we received your request for a photostatic copy of your deed we were having trouble with our copying machine. It was necessary to send the deed to an outside firm to have the copy made. Now, I'm glad to report to you that the copy was sent out yesterday by first-class mail.

We regret this inconvenience to you and trust you will understand the unavoidable delay.

Cordially,

Incoming letter

Admitting Error of Omission

Dear Mr. Moseley,

My employer, Mr. Sheldon Frank, wrote you on January 20th, and mentioned that he was enclosing half a dozen samples of the paper stock in which you were interested.

Through an oversight on my part, these samples were not enclosed. You will find them attached to this letter and I hope you have not been unduly inconvenienced by this delay.

Very truly yours,

Answering letter

Dear Miss Wimple,

We realized, of course, that the samples of paper stock were inadvertently omitted when we received Mr. Frank's letter.

Thank you so much for promptly picking up your error and sending the samples which we received yesterday.

Cordially,

Incoming letter

Unavoidable Change of Schedule

Dear Mr. Drummond,

As you know from my letter of last week, it was my intention to see you on Friday during a three-hour stopover scheduled at Kansas City.

Much to my regret, flying conditions were very, very bad over the airport and the plane skipped Kansas City entirely and went right on to Chicago.

It is my plan to make another trip out your way at the end of March. I'll drop you a line when my dates are specific and shall hope to get together with you at that time.

Meantime, if there is any information you need for your budgeting before my visit in March, just let me know and I'll do what I can to get it to you by mail. I'm so sorry I couldn't see you on this last trip.

Cordially,

Answering letter

Dear Mr. Wallace,

The storm here in Kansas City came in with such fury that we knew your plane would not be able to land—so we were not at all surprised when you didn't phone.

Since we don't plan to start sorting out figures for the new budget until some time in June, it will be quite all right to get the information we need from you in March. We shall look forward to seeing you at that time. Please let us know in advance the date of your expected arrival, and if there are any accommodations we can arrange for you, we will be glad to do so.

Cordially,

Incoming letter

Dear Mr. Shaw,

The people at Blackstone are very upset about the poor reproduction of their ad in the June issue. Can you find out what happened and what can we do about it? They will object to paying for this ad, I'm sure.

Cordially,

Answering letter

Poor Reproduction—Adjustment

Dear Mr. Feldman,

In reply to your inquiry, I have checked with Mr. Corcoran who has heard from the printer, and there is no reasonable explanation for the rather poor reproduction of the Blackstone ad in the June issue.

Like the rest of us, I guess printers just plain goof now and then. However, we will be happy to credit Blackstone with $200 to be used in connection with their next invoice, and this is the best we can do.

Incidentally, you'll be pleased to note that the ad is still pulling very well—meaning, of course, that Blackstone has not lost benefits because of this slight loss of reproduction quality.

Mr. Corcoran asks that you consult with your client and hopes you will confirm with a letter the acceptance of this credit.

Cordially,

Incoming letter

Dear Mr. Shaw,

In reference to your secretary's letter of June 7th suggesting a $200 credit for the Blackstone ad, we'd like to reach a more equitable agreement through your printer.

We feel that a 50% settlement, in credit or in advertising space, is not out of line. Since the reproduction was the error of the printer, we would assume he should accept the responsibility for making good. I hope to hear from you at your convenience.

Cordially,

Answering letter

Stressing Evidence for Adjustment

Dear Mr. Feldman,

I'm sorry to say, in reply to your June 21st letter, that there is nothing further we can do about the Blackstone dissatisfaction with reproduction. The $200 is more than I honestly believe the case warrants since the ad was certainly readable and proof of this is evident in the fact that the ad has pulled more than 800 inquiries through June 21st—more, by well over 100, *than any other ad which appeared in the June issue*.

The printer, incidentally, gave me a credit of $50, so you see I'm making every attempt to be generous.

I hope you'll explain this to your client and will understand our point of view—that the ad has carried more than its weight in spite of the slight loss of reproduction quality.

Cordially,

Incoming letter

A Luncheon Date

Dear Miss Mason,

I simply don't know how to begin this letter for, thanks be, I've never had to write a similar one. But I guess there's just no other way to do it other than to admit that I goofed (and how!).

After looking forward for nearly a month to your visit, you arrived yesterday when I was out of town. My trip was certainly unexpected and unplanned. A last-minute emergency at our Pittsburgh plant required my presence and I failed to look at my appointment calendar for Thursday before I left. In talking with my secretary on the long-distance phone that morning, she told me she had discovered I had an appointment with you for lunch that day. It was humanly impossible to get back to Louisville by noon, even via the fastest jet.

I trust you understood not only the situation but also my sincere regret. Do you think you are in a sufficiently forgiving mood to make another lunch date with me for Wednesday, the 21st? I'm so very anxious to talk with you about your new project and you have my word that, this time, I'll be "Johnny-on-the-spot."

Cordially,

Answering letter

Dear Mrs. Vandenhove,

Your secretary was so very nice about explaining your sudden trip out of town that it was impossible for me to be annoyed. I wouldn't have been anyway! These things happen occasionally.

I've marked the new date on my calendar—Wednesday, June 21st, at 12:00 noon, and I'll meet you at the Club, as usual.

Sincerely,

Incoming letter

Dear Mrs. Watson,

Six weeks ago, I ordered six dozen pamphlets called *How to Keep Expense Records for Uncle Sam*. My check for $7.20 accompanied the order and I asked for prompt delivery so I could use the pamphlets at a sales meeting scheduled for March 15th.

March 15th has come and gone and the sales meeting is over. The pamphlets have still not arrived. They're of no use to me now, so I'd like my money back as soon as possible. Will you please forward your check right away?

Cordially,

Answering letter

Suggest Another Use for Delayed Goods

Dear Mr. Lambert,

We're so sorry that the pamphlets you ordered didn't reach you in time for your sales meeting. There was delay in shipping them, since we had to go into a second printing when the demand became heavier than we expected.

The pamphlets will reach you, I'm sure, in the next day or two, and I'd like to suggest that you mail one to each of your salesmen. Though I know it would have been more effective to distribute these at your meeting, I'm sure you realize that the subject matter of this pamphlet is still important.

I hope you will agree with my suggestion and accept my apology for the delay.

Cordially,

V

Letters OF CONFIRMATION

❦ Frequently, appointments in business are made well in advance and meetings or other functions are scheduled long before they actually take place. Sometimes, too, appointments are set up verbally with the understanding that they will be confirmed in writing before they occur. Under such circumstances, a good secretary will write letters which not only verify the appointment dates but which will also serve as a reminder to the persons involved.

Frequently too, letters are written to confirm arrangements and commitments made verbally. When this is done, specific data must be clearly outlined.

CHECK LIST
FOR LETTERS OF CONFIRMATION

1. Give exact dates, prices, figures, and so forth.

2. Ask for written or phoned verification by a specific date.
3. Offer an alternate date, time or suggestion if there is any doubt that the first plans are no longer acceptable.

Incoming letter

Dear Miss Madden,

I'm most anxious to get the final figures on the costs for decorating my living and dining rooms, as well as the upholstering of the divan.

Also, please let me know when someone will be here to pick up the divan, and when the paper hanger and painters will arrive. This is most important, for with my heavy schedule I must arrange to have someone here to let them in if I'm unable to be at home at the time.

Cordially,

Answering letter

Costs and Schedule of Decorating

Dear Mrs. Bohn,

When I wrote you last week, I had not completed my estimate of costs for the decorating of your living and dining rooms, nor for the upholstering of the divan. I gave you a tentative figure for the entire job of $600. My figures are now complete and I find that the price will be slightly less than that, actually only $543.75.

We can pick up the divan next Monday, if that is agreeable, and have it completely rebuilt and re-upholstered in the fabric you selected by the time the papering and painting is done. Our paper hanger and painters will also be at your home early Monday morning, approximately 8 o'clock.

If you have any further questions before that time, or if the timing is unsatisfactory, please don't hesitate to phone me.

Cordially,

Incoming letter

Dear Mr. Denham,

When we talked on the telephone last week, you told me that you would be interested in two station wagons, if I could give you a much better price per wagon than I was able to offer you on only one.

This morning, another station wagon trade-in came in. It's a Pontiac, in excellent condition, and has belonged to one owner, a woman, since it was new in 1961. It's been beautifully cared for and has gone only a little over 10,000 miles.

If you are interested in this wagon and the other Pontiac which you looked at early last week, I can offer you the two for only $4,500. Naturally, I must have your decision at once. I shall hold the two wagons for only four days and hope to have your letter confirming the sale before the end of the week.

If you decide to take me up on this offer, will you phone me at once and tell me your letter is going into the mail? As you can understand, I must have the order in writing.

Cordially,

Answering letter

Details and Cost of Motor Vehicles

Dear Mr. Turner,

This will confirm my phone call to you this morning and constitutes my agreement to purchase the two Pontiac station wagons we talked of for a total price of $4,500. Naturally, this sale is subject to cancellation if either or both of the station wagons fail to live up to your description of them.

So let's reiterate. Pontiac station wagon Number 1, the one I saw a little over a week ago, is a 1960 model, light green, six cylinders, with approximately 17,000 miles on the speedometer. With it go two new tires, plus the two tires which are presently on the front wheels.

The second station wagon is also a Pontiac, 1961 model, with slightly over 10,000 miles on the speedometer. It is white, and with it go the four tires presently on the wheels and a brand-new spare.

I'll expect delivery next Saturday afternoon, as you promised.

Cordially,

Incoming letter

Dear Mr. Cangle,

As you know, in about two weeks we hope to place an order for 10,000 vacuum tubes for shipment to Brussels, and we need more information as quickly as you can get it to us.

Please confirm in writing the price you quoted on the telephone. Also, I need estimated shipping costs by both surface and air freight.

Cordially,

Answering letter

Cost of Merchandise and Shipping Charges Overseas

Dear Mr. Chatham,

This will confirm my quotation to you of $21,300 for 10,000 #700-3X vacuum tubes. The usual 2% discount applies for cash within 10 days. If we use air freight, the price for shipment will be $263.40. Shipment by surface would cost only $135.66, but, as I mentioned, delivery date will then be extremely uncertain and unpredictable.

If you wish to authorize immediate shipment by either method, please drop me a note at your very earliest convenience. Thank you for this business.

Cordially,

Incoming letter

Dear Miss Heller,

It was very kind of you to send the brochure showing the programs to be given by the Civic Opera Society.

In order to make my plans quickly, I need more information from you. What will the charge be for two seats, Row AA, Numbers 4 and 6, for the full season? I'll send my check promptly just as soon as I hear from you.

Cordially,

Answering letter

Details and Cost of Concert Seats

Dear Mrs. Ashworth,

Thank you so very much for your inquiry concerning a season subscription to the Civic Opera Society performances. This will confirm the availability of the two seats you prefer, Row AA, Numbers 4 and 6, for the full season. The price for the entire group of concerts will be $76, plus the usual 10% entertainment tax, or a total of $83.60. Upon receipt of your check or money order, I will forward your tickets.

Here's to an enjoyable series with us. The 1964-65 bookings should prove more exciting than anything we have done in many years.

Cordially,

Incoming letter

Dear Mr. Jacoby,

After our discussion about the position of Personnel Manager at Affiliated last Tuesday, I've thought it over carefully and I am now ready to accept your offer and will report for work on Monday the 27th, at 9:00 A.M.

In the meantime, will you be kind enough to send me a letter comfirming the points we agreed on such as salary, raises, hospitalization and the pension plan?

Thank you very much.

Cordially,

Answering letter

Agreement on Salary and Benefits

Dear Miss Patterson,

This will confirm the arrangement made Tuesday afternoon in connection with the position of Personnel Manager here at Affiliated.

The job will pay $140 a week for the first three months. There will be, provided your work is satisfactory, a ten-dollar-a-week increase, for the second three-month period. After that, your salary will be subject to frequent review and discussion.

After two months with us, you will automatically be put into our hospitalization and life insurance plan, and at the same time you may start to contribute to the pension plan, if you so desire. Details of both of these excellent fringe benefits are outlined in the booklet I gave you while you were here.

We'll expect you to report here at 9:00 A.M. next Monday, the 27th. I know you'll enjoy your work at Affiliated and we're looking forward to your arrival with great enthusiasm.

Cordially,

Incoming letter

Dear Mr. Jones,

I've had time to think about the offer you made me last Thursday and want you to know that I consider it a most attractive one. If my understanding of the various segments of the offer is correct, I'd like the job and will be free to start on Monday, September 12th.

Will you be kind enough, therefore, to confirm in writing the following items, if they are correct?

1. The job will carry the title: "Assistant to the President."
2. The duties entail a wide variety of functions, but the primary purpose of the job is to learn how management "thinks" and to help carry out these thoughts.
3. The beginning salary is $14,000 per year.
4. There is a 1% commission on company sales over and above the budgeted half-a-million dollars. This rate of commission is subject to review before the next year's budgeting period.
5. There will be a car allowance of $50 per month, plus 8 cents a mile for car travel on company business.
6. There will be a secretary assigned to assist me and she will have no other responsibilities.

Once again, thanks for the challenging offer. I'm eagerly awaiting the 12th of September, and hope to have your letter of confirmation by return mail.

Cordially,

Answering letter

Agreement on Salary and Benefits

Dear Mr. Thompson,

This will, indeed, confirm each of the factors mentioned in your recent letter. Your understanding of my offer is correct in every respect. I'm delighted to know you'll be with us shortly and look forward with great anticipation to your assistance. See you on Monday, September 12th.

Cordially,

Incoming letter

Dear Mr. Lancome,

We're glad to tell you that the plans for your research program are just about ready for us to begin the actual work. However, since our last discussion with you a week ago, we have not received the written confirmation of all the arrangements on this project.

Would you be able to get this off to us by return mail, Mr. Lancome? Thank you very much.

Cordially,

Answering letter

Agreement on Research Program

Dear Mr. Johnson,

I'm sorry there has been delay in sending you our written confirmation in connection with our research program. As you know, time is of the essence, and it's my hope that you will, upon receipt of this letter, proceed with the survey we discussed. If there are any unanswered questions or problems, please call me right away.

Very truly yours,

Incoming letter

Dear Mr. Brown,

I hope I have the places and dates properly determined. It's my understanding that we will close the matter to do with the transfer of your real estate on Elm Street at my office on Thursday, February 11th, at 9:30 A.M. Because other people are also involved, will you be good enough to have your secretary send me a confirming letter if that time and date are correct?

Cordially,

Answering letter

Change of Dates for Appointment

Dear Mr. Sedley,

Mr. Brown has asked me to write you that there must be some misunderstanding. He has arranged that he and the other persons involved will be present at your office on Wednesday, February 10th at 9:30 A.M. Will you do whatever is necessary, therefore to make this change since neither Mr. Brown nor the others can make it on the 11th?

Please phone me or drop me a note at once confirming this date, so that we're all sure there will be no one arriving on the wrong day.

Cordially,

Incoming letter

Dear Mr. Tooley,

The papers for the closing on your newly purchased property are all ready for your signature. We will expect you at our office on Maple Avenue on Tuesday, February 9th, at 10:30 A.M.

Please bring Mrs. Tooley and Mr. Zooker with you because we will need their signatures, too.

Cordially,

Answering letter

Time of Real Estate Closing

Dear Mr. Sutton,

Mr. Tooley has asked that I send you this letter of confirmation. The closing will take place, as outlined in your letter of the 17th, at your office on Tuesday, February 9th, at 10:30 A.M. Mr. Tooley and the other principals involved will be present at that time.

Cordially,

Incoming letter

Dear Mr. Johnson,

On checking my schedule further, I find that I will be able to come to your office on Wednesday, April 19th, at 11:00 A.M. as previously suggested. Will you kindly let me know if this is still convenient for you?

Cordially,

Answering letter

Secretary Confirms Time of Meeting

Dear Mr. Evans,

Before Mr. Johnson left for Chicago on Friday, he asked me to confirm in writing your appointment with him for 11:00 A.M. on Wednesday, April 19th. He'll be happy to see you here at his office at that time.

Cordially,

Incoming letter

Dear Mr. Finnegan,

There are some details which I need before we actually go ahead with the construction of the Fidelity Bank and Trust Company annex.

First of all, is it possible to make minor changes after construction gets under way where interior plans are concerned? We're completely satisfied with the exterior, so there will be no changes necessary there.

Second, just how soon will you be able to start on the annex?

Also, will you please confirm in your letter the total cost of construction and the manner in which you expect payment?

Cordially,

Answering letter

Cost of Construction and Method of Payment

Dear Mr. Crandall,

This will confirm our mutual agreement to start erection of the Fidelity Bank and Trust Company annex on Front Street as soon as possible. The annex will conform to the specifications and plans indicated on the attached blueprints, as approved by you last week.

As I told you, minor changes may be made even after construction is under way where the interior plans are concerned. The exterior must remain as indicated, so I'm glad it is satisfactory.

For your records, the total cost of construction will be $237,000. Twenty-five percent of this amount must be paid as soon as possible so that we may order some of the necessary materials. Another 25 percent will be due when the exterior construction is completed. The balance is payable upon full completion of the entire project. A cost sheet is attached. If we can place our original order for materials by Monday, May 10th, work can start on or before June 15th.

I look forward eagerly to this challenging opportunity.

Cordially,

VI

Letters OF CONGRATULATION

❦ The personal interest indicated by a letter
of congratulations makes this sort of a letter
extremely worthwhile. Occasions for congratulations in business and socially are innumerable.
Take advantage of these opportunities. Flowery
or syrupy phrasing is taboo; it smacks of in-
sincerity. The best rules to remember in connection with congratulatory letters are those
of warmth and naturalness.

CHECK LIST
FOR LETTERS OF CONGRATULATION

1. Be enthusiastic and friendly.
2. Be sincere and show no envy.
3. Say nothing that will detract from the
   accomplishment or occasion which deserves congratulation.

Incoming letter

Dear Mr. Hammer,

Enclosed is a clipping of the announcement of the recent marriage of P. S. Hampden and the young lady he has been seen with for the past year. I thought that perhaps you and others at the office would like to know about this happy event, so that you could get a note of congratulations into the mail.

Cordially,

Answering letter

On a Marriage—Business

Dear Mr. Hampden,

A clipping of the announcement of your recent marriage was sent to me by our mutual friend John Pawling. May I offer my sincerest congratulations and best wishes to you and your bride?

Cordially,

Incoming letter

Dear George and Grace,

This little note brings you the wonderful news of my marriage to John Hathaway right here in romantic Madrid. The clipping, which I am enclosing, gives the details of the wedding so beautifully that I will not attempt to write more.

Affectionately,

Answering letter

On a Marriage—a Close Friend

Dear Marion,

Grace and I were so pleased to receive your note enclosing the newspaper clipping telling of your marriage to John Hathaway. Even though the wedding took place in Madrid, we shall drink to your happiness and joy. Grace is popping the champagne cork right this minute. Here's to you—Marion and John!

Our very best wishes to you, always,

Incoming letter

Dear Mr. Wilson,

Did you happen to notice in the *Review* this morning that Mr. and Mrs. H. W. Conway became the proud parents of a boy? They have named him Joseph. Just thought you'd want to know.

Cordially,

Answering letter

On a Birth—Business

Dear Mr. Conway,

Becoming a parent is one of the greatest thrills in the world! Believe me, I know—I'm the father of four. Sincerest congratulations to you and Mrs. Conway on the birth of Joseph.

I hope we can see him soon.

Sincerely,

Incoming letter

Dear Harry,

Alice has sent off the pretty blue announcements—but as I promised you before I left the office on Wednesday, I wanted you to hear the good news from me, too. I'm sure when you see little Joe, you'll agree with me that he is the most wonderful baby ever.

Cordially,

Answering letter

On a Birth—A Close Friend

Dear Joe,

Welcome to the club! I was so pleased this morning to receive the announcement of the birth of little Joe and then to get your note in the second mail. I know how proud you and Alice must be. Do let me know when you're ready to show him off. Mary and I want to see him—and his parents—as soon as possible. My sincerest congratulations.

As ever,

Incoming letter

Political Success

My dear Governor,

I was very glad to learn from a mutual friend, Chuck Davis, late last night that you will be our next Governor. I have long been one of your ardent supporters and I know you will make an excellent chief-of-state.

In my small way, I'll be ever so pleased to help in any way I can. I'm willing to serve on any committee where you might find my background useful. And if an introductory tea or cocktail party might further your popularity in Menwell County, my home is available for that purpose, too. Just say the word!

Cordially,

Answering letter

Dear Mr. Harrington,

Thank you very much for your kind letter of good wishes. I think some sort of a social gathering in Menwell County would be very timely and is an excellent idea. I'd like to meet as many people who helped with the campaign as I possibly can. I'll have Miss Thompson, my secretary, get in touch with you to get plans under way. You are very thoughtful to have made the suggestion.

Cordially,

Incoming letter

On a Promotion

Dear Mr. Smith,

It didn't take the Gans Company long to recognize your true worth. Ten years is an extremely short time in which to run the full length of the course—from junior salesman to vice-president. You've worked hard, I know, and the new title is more than deserved. I hope it makes you even happier, however, to realize that all of us here at the midwestern division are delighted that you have been properly rewarded. And our cooperation is yours—even without the asking.

Cordially,

Answering letter

Dear Mr. Silverman,

Your letter of congratulations arrived just a few hours after Mr. Smith left for Milwaukee on an extended business trip. In the meantime I want to thank you for him, and I will forward your letter to him tomorrow.

Cordially,

Incoming letter

On a Promotion

Dear Ridge,

I know how happy you and Suzanne must be at the news of your promotion. The step forward is well deserved and I'm sure your new duties will prove challenging. My very best wishes to you.

Cordially,

Answering letter

Dear Henry,

Suzanne and I are about ready to burst out with joy over the promotion. As you know, I did spend considerable overtime on the last survey—but it has paid off. Thank you very much for your good wishes.

Cordially,

Incoming letter

On a New Job

Dear Mr. Hall,

The day of parting has come—a mighty big day in your life! And though I hate to see you leave this organization of which you have been such an important part, I want you to know that our very best wishes for your further success go with you. The Planter Company is lucky, indeed, to have you go over to their side.

Sincerely,

Answering letter

Dear Mr. Hatfield,

I'm sorry that I did not get to see you personally to thank you for your note before I left the office last week. Coming here to The Planter Company was a lucky break for me because I felt I had served my usefulness with Gardner Co. However, I do want you to know that I will always remember your kindness and generosity as a fellow-worker for the past five years. You helped to make my stay at Gardner a pleasant one, indeed.

Cordially,

Incoming letter

On a New Job

Dear Mr. Crown,

I read in yesterday's paper about your new appointment and want to tell you how pleased I was. I'm sure your very real and experienced capabilities in the field of merchandising will prove to be just what the Hunneker Company needs to retain its position of leadership. Lots of success and happiness in the new job.

Cordially,

Answering letter

Dear Mr. Johnson,

Thank you so much for your letter of good wishes which was on my desk when I arrived at my office this morning. I can assure you that I will do my best to prove worthy of this opportunity.

Cordially,

Incoming letter

Dear Mrs. Hepplewhite,

Under separate cover, I'm sending a copy of my new book. I hope you will have the time to read it right away; I am so anxious to know your reaction.

Cordially,

Answering letter

On a Book

Dear Mr. Kennedy,

Your new book came this morning and now, at four in the afternoon, I had to make myself put it down. The story is fascinating, your style really delightful. I've only another 30 or 40 pages to go and I've decided to wind up with the happy ending (I hope!) just before bedtime tonight.

Best wishes for the book's success. Such a fine piece of work just can't miss!

Cordially,

Incoming letter

Personal Achievement—Business

Dear Mr. Ramsdell,

You must be, indeed, proud to know that you have headed up the Trent Corporation for 30 productive years. The company's growth has been one of those exciting success stories one hears about all too seldom, and I know that a large measure of the responsibility and decision-making was yours.

Not only, therefore, do I congratulate you for your achievements in the past but I look forward with you to even greater accomplishments in the years ahead.

Cordially,

Answering letter

Dear Mr. Waters,

Thank you for your kindness in sending congratulations to me for my 30th anniversary here. Time has gone by all too swiftly, and I'm sure I have not done enough—there is still so much to do!

Cordially,

Incoming letter

On Receipt of an Award

Dear Colonel,

On behalf of the whole group here at Pioneer, I want to congratulate you most sincerely upon your being awarded the Overseas Press Club medal of honor.

It's very inspiring to all of your former co-workers here

to know of your excellent performance and fine record achieved in the reporting of news from overseas in these strategic times when accurate reporting is so vital.

We understand that you're due shortly for a leave at home. If you can spare the time, we'd like it so much if you can stop in at the office and let us congratulate you personally.

Cordially,

Answering letter

Dear Mr. Golden,

Your thoughtfulness in sending congratulations from Pioneer is indeed appreciated. I remember so well all the effort on your part to teach me to do the job as it should be done, and I want to thank you for all you did for me while I was working at the plant.

My leave will start in about a month and you can be sure that I've scheduled Pioneer as one of the places I will visit without fail.

Cordially,

Incoming letter

Personal Achievement

Dear Don,

Brad had mentioned your newest invention to me some time ago and I was delighted to read a clipping he sent today that you have secured the patent on it.

It'll be fun in the years to come to be able to say to my children—and yours—"I knew him when—."

I hope the patent will bring you the full measure of success and approbation you so richly deserve.

Sincerely,

Answering letter

Dear Hal,

It was good of Brad to bring you up to date about the patent on my latest invention, and I want to thank you for your congratulations. The work on this bearing was so time-consuming and aggravating at times that it seems almost impossible to believe that the job is finally completed. Naturally, I'm now hoping it will be useful to others by the million!

Cordially,

Incoming letter

80th Birthday

Dear Dr. Miller,

I'm writing this letter with the thought that you might like to know that Dr. John Sutherland, chairman of the Cleveland Division of the A.M.A., will celebrate his eightieth birthday next Sunday.

Your name, of course, will appear on the list of A.M.A. members who wish him well in an official manner, as is our custom. However, I thought you might like to send him a word of personal greeting, too. Hence this reminder.

Cordially,

Answering letter

80th Birthday

Dear John,

A little bird—whose name is Miss Alice Brothers—has tipped me off to the fact that you will enter octagenaria on Sunday next.

I am most grateful to Miss Brothers, for had she not revealed that this will be your eightieth birthday, I would have guessed you were hitting sixty-five or so and, please believe me, this is no attempt at flattery.

An eightieth birthday, in my book, I assure you, deserves special notice and attention. I do hope you will have an extremely happy anniversary.

Cordially,

Incoming letter

THE FACTS—FOR YOUR EVALUATION

For the first eight months of the year, *High Fidelity's* rates were based on an average monthly circulation of 110,-000. In other words, you bought and paid for a total of 880,000 primary reader impressions during that period. But, as the attached *High Fidelity* Publisher's Statements will show, we actually delivered to you a total of 915,456 impressions— a bonus of 35,456 reader impressions. And for the last four months, when our rates were based on an average of 115,000, we delivered a total of 470,460 primary reader impressions, or an additional bonus of 10,460 impressions over and above the 460,000 for which you paid—*a total bonus of 45,916 for the year.*

Just thought you'd want to know.

Cordially,

Answering letter

Sales Ability

Dear Mrs. Eddings,

Congratulations on your letter of April 3rd, "THE FACTS —FOR YOUR EVALUATION."

To us, this is real "creative selling" and we certainly appreciate it.

Of course, we could (and frequently do) work out these figures—but we compliment you on having done it. As you say, you have stated the facts!

That's why we prefer a simple, full-of-facts letter to the fanciest brochure in the world.

Sincerely,

Incoming letter

Civic Affairs

Dear Chris,

It was with much pleasure that I read this morning of the honors paid to you yesterday by the Urban Renewal League of Greater New York. May I add my congratulations to the many I'm sure you've received?

It gives one a feeling of confidence in the many urban renewal programs which are now under way to know that experts like you, with real concern for the beauty and balanced design of such necessary adjuncts to progress as the modern turnpike, are being formally recognized for these very attributes.

I hope when the time comes for Great Neck (that's where I live, you know) to renew itself, we'll be fortunate enough to enjoy the kind of planning that earned the Urban Renewal League honors for you. Would you have any objection to my putting your name before the Great Neck board of selectmen?

Cordially,

Answering letter

Dear Mal,

Thank you very much for your kind letter and congratulations on the honors paid me by the Urban Renewal League. It was a fine day and a most interesting program. I'm sorry that you weren't there.

Any time you let me know, I'll be more than happy to come out for a session with your board of selectmen. Since my schedule is pretty heavy these days, could you give me a choice of two or three dates?

Kindest regards and best wishes.

Cordially,

Incoming letter

Civic Affairs

To the Editor

Dear Sir,

Congratulations to the police of Fairhaven for the quick arrest of the resident who neglected to take his refuse to the local dump or otherwise dispose of it.

Now it will be interesting to see if our courts will uphold this arrest with a conviction. I think it is only through an example of this sort that we will ever clean up the residential areas where filth and neglect are so rampant.

In a town like Fairhaven, slums can develop far too quickly. A resident has a duty not only to himself but to his neighbors to avoid any carelessness which can harm the health of his fellow citizens. He has a fair enough choice where garbage accumulation is concerned. If he doesn't want to spend the money to have his garbage collected by a commercial collector, he can lug it to the dump himself.

Either way, garbage must go! A few arrests like this recent one, and it doesn't seem to me that there will be much "old" garbage left around.

Very truly yours,

Answering letter

Dear Mr. Smith,

It was gratifying to read your letter in last night's *Herald*. The boys on the force join me in saying "Thank You" for your support of our efforts to enforce the law. We don't often see such praise in print.

Cordially,

VII

Letters OF COMPLAINT

✎ Though promptness is an essential of all business correspondence, there is no situation that requires more promptness than when a letter of complaint is received. Even if the complaint must be studied, and satisfaction (or adjustment) cannot be immediately accomplished, the letter of complaint demands an immediate reply.

There are several important rules to remember when responding to a letter of complaint.

CHECK LIST
FOR LETTERS OF COMPLAINT

1. Try to put yourself in the complainant's shoes.
2. Don't belittle the complaint. The writer thinks it's a serious matter or he wouldn't have written.

3. Admit guilt, where necessary, and then try to make amends.

Incoming letter

Unsatisfactory Merchandise—Infraction of Guarantee

Dear Sir,

In February, I ordered a manifold antenna from one of your San Francisco dealers.

The literature which accompanied the antenna stated that full satisfaction is guaranteed. I regret to tell you that the antenna did not improve my reception, so I returned it to the dealer who refused to refund my money, but insisted on giving me a credit toward another purchase, which I have no intention of making.

I think this is a deliberate infraction of the guarantee you offer. If you agree, will you please see what you can do to obtain satisfaction for me? The dealer is Mugford Music at 10 Pacific Drive.

An early reply will be very much appreciated.

Very truly yours,

Answering letter

Dear Mr. Dean,

Thanks very much for your recent letter and for calling this important matter to my attention.

I'm investigating this situation and hope to have some word for you shortly. I intend to straighten it out to your complete satisfaction.

In the meantime, I wonder if you can send me your bill of sale on the Strandenburg antenna. This will help me by giving model number, date of purchase, etc.

Cordially,

Incoming letter

Inferior Merchandise

Dear Sir,

On July 2nd, I purchased an overstuffed chair at your store. The chair was delivered on July 5th and we have used it in our home for less than a month. Already, the webbing underneath has given way and the springs are starting to drop down so that they are now visible beneath the chair when it is upright. Naturally, because of this, the cushion has become indented, and the chair looks like it has been around and subject to hard use for many, many years.

It does not seem possible that a brand-new chair, used in the most ordinary and limited fashion for less than a month, should be in such condition—especially when it cost me $240.

I'd like to return the chair to you for either replacement with one that lives up to its price tag or a full rebate. Please contact me immediately on receipt of this letter.

Sincerely,

Answering letter

Dear Mr. Bourke,

We are very sorry to learn that the chair you purchased from us seems to be of inferior quality, and we have notified the manufacturer of your dissatisfaction. We certainly want you to be happy with purchases from Dunn's and our merchandise is fully guaranteed on a money-back basis.

On the enclosed card, will you kindly indicate the time and date when it will be convenient to have this chair picked up and returned? Also, will you let us know on line 2 of the card if you wish to choose a replacement or prefer the $240 credited to your account? The card is directed to our

Mr. Tanglewood on the third floor and he will be happy to assist you in any way if you wish to come in and look at chairs made by other manufacturers.

We are extremely sorry for the inconvenience caused you. This is one of those rare instances where a normally excellent house has had the misfortune to turn out an unsatisfactory piece of furniture.

Thank you for calling the matter to our attention.

Cordially,

Incoming letter

Defective Merchandise

Dear Mr. Scott,

A phone call to Smith & Sentry the other day indicated that you are the man to whom I must complain. And complain is putting it mildly. Since when does a can of S & S peaches include a rusty nail, and for free? That's exactly what I bit into the other morning when I tackled my breakfast, which unfortunately consisted of peaches from this particular can.

I was lucky. I bit down on the nail, but did no damage to my teeth or mouth. Fortunately, I didn't swallow it either. However, it seems to me that you had better keep an eye on what goes into your cans, besides peaches, from now on. Somebody else might be more inclined to sue you than I am.

The nail, none the worse for wear, is enclosed for your scrutiny. It's a peach, isn't it?

Cordially,

Answering letter

Dear Mr. Schenkel,

I was expecting your letter after a phone call reporting the ghastly details of the rusty nail found in the can of peaches bearing the label of Smith & Sentry, Inc.

Thank you for calling this to our attention. As you can imagine, we are grateful that you suffered no serious injury, and we wish to extend our apologies for this unpleasant and potentially dangerous experience.

We are taking additional precautions to make certain that such an incident does not occur again. Please accept my sincerest regrets.

Cordially,

Incoming letter

Billed for Goods Not Ordered

Dear Sirs,

Your September statement of our account shows a charge of $417.77 for a shipment of nylon net made on August 10th. We have not ordered any nylon net from you at any time, nor have we received such a shipment.

There is doubtless some sort of a clerical error here, but I would appreciate your prompt investigation and an immediate cancellation of the charges against us. We will need your credit memo for this amount or a revised statement, whichever is preferable.

Very truly yours,

Answering letter

Dear Mr. Meyer,

The error in your September statement showing a charge of $417.77 for a shipment of nylon net was due to the fact that our regular billing clerk was suddenly taken ill and we had to call in an inexperienced substitute to complete her work.

We are very sorry to have inconvenienced you, and a credit memo for the above amount is enclosed.

Cordially,

Incoming letter

Billed for Merchandise Previously Returned

Dear Mr. Hayes,

An old customer is a good customer—and I think I qualify on both counts. I've been dealing with your store for some 27 years, since I was 18, as a matter of fact. My first charge account was at Bloom's. Your records will show that I've done my full share of charging—and my payments have always been prompt.

I think this is my first letter of complaint to you in all these years. That doesn't mean that your services have been perfect. It does mean, however, that never before have I felt strongly enough about a grievance to put it in writing.

Now I simply *must* let you have it! In April, I purchased and charged to my account one portable television set—price $199.50. In spite of your sales clerk's assurance that it needed no rooftop antenna, it simply didn't operate when we plugged it in. Your maintenance man came in and very quickly informed me that this model couldn't be used in our part of town without an antenna.

Your truckman kindly picked up the television set and I assume he returned it to your store or warehouse. He gave me the attached memo for credit.

I'm still being billed—every month since May, and here we are in October—for the television set which has been back in your possession for six months. My letters to your billing department have had no effect.

Now I'm insisting, Mr. Hayes, that you as president of Bloom's put a stop to this undeserved and continuous billing in my name. If *you* can't do it, perhaps I will have to think about a "defamation of credit" law suit.

This isn't the way my mind usually works. Surely you won't force me to such a drastic about-face.

Cordially,

Answering letter

Dear Mr. Mackay,

It's easy enough to understand your present frame of mind about Bloom's. Please accept my abject apologies.

Our Billing Department most certainly threw a curve. Some odd and unaccountable activity on the part of our new billing computer—a strange and mighty machine which is wondrous to behold but occasionally mysterious in its performance—must be blamed. We've pressed a whole new set of buttons now, and can assure you that you won't be bothered with this matter again.

Thanks so much for your patience.

Cordially,

Incoming letter

Incorrect Billing

Dear Mr. Solow,

The December statement on Mrs. Frederick Waller's account appears to be incorrect. The previous balance due was, according to Mrs. Waller's records, only $9.80, but the current statement shows this balance as $98.00.

Will you please make a correction in your books and send a revised statement to Mrs. Waller at your early con-

venience? As soon as the revised bill is received, Mrs. Waller
will send you a check in payment of the account in full.

Very truly yours,

Answering letter

Dear Mr. Waller,

Thank you for calling our attention to the error in
Mrs. Waller's account. It has been corrected and a revised
bill will be sent to Mrs. Waller within the next few days.
Please extend our apologies to Mrs. Waller.

Cordially,

Incoming letter

Error in Bank Statement

Dear Sirs,

Today I received my checking account monthly statement covering deposits and withdrawals for the month of
January.

There is evidently a great deal of confusion about this
account and I hope you will immediately recheck your figures.
My records show two deposits of $194.00 each, one made
on January 3rd, and the other on January 17th. Each of
these deposits show up on your statement as $149.00.

Also, a cancelled check was included with the statement
for $71.05, made out to The Page Company and dated De-
cember 17th. However, the statement shows this amount to
be $71.50. Will you please check this figure, also? If neces-
sary, I'll be glad to bring my statement and cancelled checks
into the bank.

These changes show my bank balance, as of January 31st, to be $817.00. I'd like verification of these figures, please.

Very truly yours,

Answering letter

Dear Mr. Honest,

The day before we received your letter, our accounting department discovered the errors in your January statement. We are now in the process of making up a revised copy of the statement and it will be mailed to you today.

It won't be necessary for you to bring the incorrect statement or the cancelled checks to the bank, since the errors are being corrected. Thank you for your cooperation and understanding.

Cordially,

Incoming letter

Obnoxious Salesman

Dear Mr. Lockwood,

I want you to know that the door to this office is no longer open to your salesman Jerry McDermott. Mr. Mc-Dermott seems to think he knows more about running our business than do we. He has, over a period of many months, come back time and time again to present a series of ridiculous schemes designed to getting us to purchase one of your high-priced computers. We don't need one of your computers, don't want one of your computers, and more particularly, don't want further contact with your Mr. Mc-Dermott.

Very truly yours,

Answering letter

Dear Mr. Fenton,

I am very sorry to learn that our salesman Jerry McDermott has become something of a nuisance in trying to convince you that you should buy one of our computers, when you have no need for one.

It is rather difficult for me to understand Mr. McDermott's high pressure approach in selling; he is probably more experienced than anyone else in this field and understands all the problems faced by people in the paper business today. We have never had reason to question his ability to sell all through the 15 years he has been with the company. However, I have asked him not to call on you again.

In the event that your business continues to grow—and I have no doubt that it will—please keep us in mind whenever you feel that our Acme Computer would be useful to you. I will be glad to call on you personally to explain all the details to you.

Cordially,

Incoming letter

Misunderstanding on Plan of Payment

Dear Mr. Trainor,

The snide letter we received from your Credit Department this morning has not only rubbed me the wrong way in connection with the invoice under discussion, but has made me decide I just don't want to do any more business with a company like yours. Your competitors will be happy to work with us on the same terms I proposed to you.

Very truly yours,

Answering letter

Dear Mr. Poponce,

You are *so* right! That letter from our Credit Department, a carbon copy of which just reached my desk, was the kind of a form letter we sometimes use where a company is neglecting its obligations to us by completely ignoring our repeated invoices. But I think I'm to blame in a way.

My letter to the Credit Department, outlining your proposal for monthly installment payments, apparently went astray, and they have not received it in Cincinnati. By phone this morning, after learning that, I detailed the proposal to them. As I assured you last week, they are more than happy to cooperate. If you will just sign the attached contract for payment and attach to it your first monthly check, we'll be off to a running start. By the way, Mr. Ryan, Credit Manager, says to call him collect if you want to discuss this arrangement in any further detail.

Please accept my sincere apologies for the receipt of a letter which was totally unwarranted and undeserved.

Cordially,

Incoming letter

Misunderstanding as to Plan of Payment

Dear Mr. Peters,

Yesterday I received your invoice #3011, dated January 8th, in the amount of $377.50. It was my understanding that the paper we bought from you would be billed at a

10 percent discount. Will you please ask your Billing Department, therefore, to cancel this invoice and issue a new one at the proper amount?

Very truly yours,

Answering letter

Dear Mr. Madison,

As your letter of the 10th pointed out, our invoice #3011 was in error. The 10 percent discount most certainly applies in this case, as Mr. Peters promised. A revised invoice will be sent to you shortly. Please excuse the mistake and thank you very much for calling it to our attention.

Very truly yours,

Incoming letter

Objection to Advertised Price

Dear Mr. Henner,

Recently you advertised blankets on sale for approximately 30 percent below their normal price. I ordered and received two of the blankets and felt completely satisfied with my purchase.

In shopping yesterday, I found the same blankets—made by the same company and with the same contents—on sale everywhere else I went at only $4 more than your sale price. It's obvious that your price was, therefore, only about 6 percent under the ordinary price.

You say that you won't be undersold on your special prices. If that's true, you'll want to send me a refund check in the amount of $11. The invoice covering the blankets I purchased from you is enclosed. Please return it to me with your check.

Cordially,

Answering letter

Dear Mrs. Ledbetter,

Our policy not to be undersold has built our business to the extent that our sales are 25 percent higher than any other store in this huge city. The policy is your guarantee that you must be satisfied with any merchandise purchased from us, both as to quality and price.

Upon investigation, we find that the wrong advertisement was run on Thursday morning last week but that the error was caught and corrected for the afternoon papers. In the meantime the comparison shoppers from competitive stores were on hand to take advantage of this situation.

Please accept our apologies for any inconvenience we have caused you; enclosed is our check for $11.

Cordially,

Incoming letter

Damaged Goods

Dear Mr. Nelson,

On December 18th, the postman on this route delivered to us two packages, mailing slips for which are enclosed. Both of these packages, sent parcel post first-class, were received in shocking condition. The outer wrappings were torn and mutilated, the inner contents were soiled. It would seem that someone ripped these packages open and then dragged them through the mud.

Though neither package was insured, first-class postage is sufficient for due care to have been exercised in treatment by post office employees. The contents of the packages were for resale, but it is absolutely out of the question for us to sell goods in such condition.

The packages and their contents are available for your inspection here. After you have examined them, I'm sure you will want to make some compensation to us.

Cordially,

Answering letter

Dear Mr. McIntosh,

We are very sorry to learn of the condition of your packages when they were delivered to you.

The Post Office Department is not liable for damages unless packages are properly insured but we will try to trace the source of the damage if it is possible to do so.

Therefore, will you kindly fill out the enclosed form and return it to us promptly?

Cordially,

Incoming letter

Service

Dear Sirs,

Attached is a photostat of a letter from a Mr. Wilson, complaining about your service. I must admit that I think he has a justifiable complaint.

Will you please contact him as soon as possible to straighten out this unhappy matter? Also, will you bring me up to date on what steps you've taken to regain Mr. Wilson's good will?

Cordially,

Answering letter

Dear Mr. Case,

Thank you for sending the photostatic copy of Mr. Wilson's letter directly to me. I agree with you that Mr. Wilson has cause for complaint, and we will do everything in our power to correct this evident error on the part of Discount Stores.

Since we want to straighten out this matter and be of future service to Mr. Wilson, I'm sending my associate Mr. Robert Powers out on Monday to see what can be done for Mr. Wilson, and also we are exploring the means to prevent such an occurrence in the future.

Cordially,

VIII

Letters OF APPRECIATION

❧ Sometimes, in the hustle and bustle of the business world, we forget that we're dealing with human beings who like to receive recognition for a job well done and appreciation for favors and services rendered. The brief phrase "thank you," warmly and sincerely offered, is always a welcome and winning way to make and keep business friendships. The letter of thanks or appreciation, therefore, ranks high in order of importance. Writing such letters doesn't require great skill, nor do letters of this kind need to be lengthy. Sometimes a hand-scrawled "you did a *swell* job!" will fill the bill. At other times, a more formal approach is preferable. The vice-president of a well-known investment company told the author that he makes it a rule to seek out occasions which can benefit from the letter of appreciation. He writes some 20 or 30 of these every week.

CHECK LIST
FOR LETTERS OF APPRECIATION

1. Write warmly and sincerely.
2. Don't write in too flowery a fashion.
3. Tell why the deed or accomplishment is so much appreciated.
4. Encourage further "unusual" performance and create the desire to again draw forth appreciation.

Incoming letter

Dear Jack,

With this letter I'm sending the six layouts for your next advertising campaign. It took a little longer than I had anticipated, but I believe that we've come up with something that will really bring in the sales. I hope you will think so too, Jack.

Cordially,

Answering letter

For Advertising Layouts

Dear Jacques,

Clients are known to be cold-blooded, unappreciative fish, who only seem happy when they're being obnoxiously critical. And because I've done my share of fault-finding, I hope you won't fall over backward in a dead faint when you receive this letter.

I simply want you to know what an excellent and artistic job I think you've done in the series of ads you've prepared for our forthcoming new campaign.

You have maximized the use of full color with your excellent sense of balance and design. The uncluttered look adds immensely, though subtly, to the message we're trying to get across.

Thanks a million, Jacques, for doing such an excellent job.

Sincerely,

Incoming letter

Dear Manny,

The 1964 *Annual Stockholders' Report* for the Bennington Division was completed last week, and I'm enclosing a copy for you. I'm as pleased with the final figures as I know you will be.

As for 1965—I would like to discuss several points with you. How about meeting me for lunch at the Pierre at 1:00 P.M. on Thursday the 26th?

Cordially,

Answering letter

Stockholders' Report

Dear Eric,

Just a quick note to compliment you most sincerely on the excellent showing you made in 1964. Your stockholders' report was just received. The Bennington Division, as you probably know by now, took top honors for the year in the area of production cost savings.

It is only through the devotion and persistence of the foundry chief that such an accomplishment can come about. What miracles are you planning for 1965? I'm looking forward to hearing about them on the 26th. One o'clock lunch at the Pierre is fine. See you then.

Sincerely,

Incoming letter

Dear Gene,

Enclosed is a carbon copy of a letter I sent off to Dan Beale yesterday. I believe we've finally "hit the nail on the head," and this letter should bring in the business you've been looking for.

Cordially,

Answering letter

For Sales Letter

Dear Harold,

Thanks for writing that splendid letter to Dan Beale. Your carbon copy came in yesterday and as I read it I realized that I've never seen the story of our product line more clearly and interestingly told. If there's an order to be had from Beale's company, this letter will bring it in.

Sincerely,

Incoming letter

Dear Joyce,

Bob and I are delighted to learn from Grace that you are about to return to your desk, and the monotony of those long weeks of convalescence will soon be only a memory.

Unless you are otherwise involved, we'd like to stop by to see you on Sunday afternoon, just to check on you to see if you are okay. Please let us know if there is anything we can do for you in the meantime.

Lovingly,

Answering letter

After Illness

Dear Helen and Bob,

When one is terribly ill, I don't suppose it matters much what day it is, but when one is lying in bed surveying a bandaged foot and suffering absolutely no pain, the time certainly does seem to drag. Your friendly visits and frequent cheerful messages did much to keep me from being bored to extinction.

I'm glad (yes, I said "glad") to be back at the old grind and I want you to know how much you helped brighten my horizon the last several weeks. Do stop in on Sunday.

Affectionately,

Incoming letter

Dear Mr. Anderson,

It was with a feeling of great shock and distress that I read of Jim Thompson's untimely death. His kindness and thoughtfulness in his dealings with others will make him stand out in my memory for a long, long time.

If there is anything we can do for you or his other associates, please do not hesitate to call me.

Sincerely,

Answering letter

For Note of Sympathy—Business

Dear Mr. Brown,

We at the Hill Company appreciate your very kind message of sympathy at the loss of our friend and co-worker

Jim Thompson. His death was a blow from which it will take some time to recover. For years, as you know, Jim was keenly involved in the progress and growth of our firm.

Thank you very much for letting us know how you felt about him.

Cordially,

Incoming letter

Dear Mr. West,

We were honored, indeed, when you asked us to show you through our plant and administrative offices on your recent visit to Copenhagen. The exchange of ideas on assembly-line efficiency was most interesting and we're seriously considering the adoption of a few of your suggestions.

Mrs. Desmond and I enjoyed very much having you dine with us, and she joins me in sending our best wishes to you and your family.

Cordially,

Answering letter

After a Foreign Visit—Business

Dear Mr. Desmond,

There was considerable delay in my return from Europe because of a storm in Genoa and the rough crossing. This is the first day back at my desk and, busy as it is, I cannot let another hour go by without thanking you for your kind letter which arrived here before I did. I also want you to know that I appreciate very much your thoughtfulness in rearranging your plans at such short notice in order to show me through your plant and administrative offices while I was in Copenhagen.

I hope some day soon you'll journey over here and give me a chance not only to take you on a tour of the Newark branch factory, but also to reciprocate with a dinner which will have to really reach out to come up to the superb quality of the one I enjoyed with you and your charming wife.

Cordially,

Incoming letter

Dear Mary,

Knowing how much you are interested in community affairs, I knew you would enjoy sitting with my committee when we met with the Savannah Club for luncheon last Thursday.

I'm enclosing a copy of the program which I think you might like to keep as a memento.

Affectionately,

Answering letter

After a Club Luncheon

Dear Louise,

Thank you so much for sending the program. I enjoyed my luncheon with the members of the Savannah Club very, very much. The food was excellent, the program itself extremely interesting, and the company most stimulating.

Will you please extend to all the members my sincere appreciation for their kindly welcome and their friendly invitation to come again? *That* I plan to do, as soon as possible.

Cordially,

Incoming letter

Dear Mrs. Jervis,

   I enjoyed your visit on Tuesday and hope that I gave you a clear answer about your insurance coverage.

   I believe so heartily in this new plan that I hope you won't let too much time elapse before making your decision.

Cordially,

Answering letter.

About Insurance Coverage

Dear Miss Forman,

   It's hard to put into words our sincere appreciation for your helpfulness in straightening out the matter of our insurance coverage.

   All that fine print is certainly confusing to the average layman and we are definitely no exception. Having you sit down with us and explain it so thoroughly has made it possible for us to realize that we definitely need more coverage in certain areas.

   We'll be in touch with you shortly, to see if we can work out a plan whereby we can afford to increase the face value of our policies.

Cordially,

Incoming letter

Dear Muriel,

   I remembered that you asked if you could attend the next Buyers' Symposium and so I'm enclosing the first invitation which came across my desk this morning. I hope to see you there.

Cordially,

Answering letter

Invitation to Symposium—Business

Dear Mr. Gonset,

It was thoughtful of you to send me an invitation to the Buyers' Symposium and I enjoyed the first session immensely. I hope I can attend the entire sequence because much can be learned, I am sure.

Sincere thanks for including me.

Cordially,

Incoming letter

Dear Mary,

I'm sending your "specs" with this note by first class mail so that they will be at your house when you get there. You left them by the swimming pool and I know how much you need them out in the sun.

It was great fun having you and John with us. Please come again soon.

Lovingly,

Answering letter

For Hospitality and Forgotten Articles

Dear Alice and Bob,

Thanks for sending Mary's glasses. I know what a nuisance it is when people forget things, but the "girls" were so busy chatting, I'm not surprised something was left behind.

We're both still talking about our swell weekend with you. Your home is charming. The buffet supper Saturday night, when we met all your friends, was just great and the companionship throughout the entire weekend was particularly enjoyable.

Mary is mailing a little parcel from Martin's—a slight token of our sincere appreciation as well as "something" she thinks Alice will consider just right for that Italian marble-topped table in the den.

Thanks again for your gracious hospitality,

Cheerio!

Incoming letter

Gentlemen,

Will you kindly send catalog and price sheets on the set of matched luggage as shown in the attached clipping from the January issue of *House and Travel* Magazine? My address is shown above.

I'd appreciate a prompt reply since we are leaving for Canada on the 18th and if we decide on the luggage we'll want it delivered before that date.

Sincerely,

Answering letter

More Information About Advertised Merchandise

Dear Mrs. Smith,

We want to thank you for the opportunity to serve you. The catalog and price sheets you requested will be mailed today under separate cover. After you've had a chance to study them, please feel free to call upon me for any additional information you may need. In the meantime, you'll be pleased to know that should you decide to order the deluxe Model 1780 set of matched luggage, we can fill your order promptly and the luggage can be in your possession at least one week before the date of your departure.

Cordially,

Incoming letter

Dear Mr. James,

Enclosed is a clipping of the column about the current Presidential campaign written by Mr. Peabody. This appeared in last Thursday's paper, and I am sending it to you in case it was not brought to your attention. Mr. Peabody would appreciate any comments you may have to make after reading the column.

Cordially,

Answering letter

Political—News Column

Dear Mr. Peabody,

I don't usually have time, nor even the inclination, to write fan letters. But I feel it is only fair to let you know how very much I enjoyed reading your Thursday evening column about the current Presidential campaign. Your secretary was kind enough to send me a clipping.

Your writings have made it clear that you're an avowed Democrat. Yet your integrity couldn't permit you to swallow some of the inaccuracies that are being bruited about, and most indiscriminately, by some of the Democratic campaigners. You are not, thank heavens, so close to the forest that you cannot see the trees.

My sincere congratulations for this far too rare example of factual reporting.

Cordially,

Incoming letter

Dear Mr. Westfield,

Mr. Desmond is out of town for the week, but he asked me to send you the clipping of his column which appeared in last Sunday's *Express*. He really was favorably impressed with your new book and feels certain that it will be the success you've hoped for.

Cordially,

Answering letter

For a Book Review

Dear Mr. Desmond,

Just a hasty note to thank you for your most complimentary mention of my book in your column last Sunday. The fact that the book has earned your attention and favorable evaluation will do much to enhance its saleability. This makes me almost as happy as it will make my publishers. If you're ever in this neck of the woods, I'd like to shake hands and say "thanks" in person.

Cordially,

Incoming letter

Dear Mr. Charles,

I know you'll be happy to have the news confirmed, even though I told you how promising it seemed when I saw you last Thursday. I talked with Mr. Kinne that same day and he asked me to write you that the Board had approved your raise, to start with the week of the 17th of July.

Cordially,

Answering letter

For Salary Increase

Dear Mr. Koch,

Thank you so very much! A salary increase is always welcome, not only from a monetary point of view but also because it gives an employee assurance that he is performing his job in a satisfactory fashion. This particular increase couldn't have come through at a nicer, more opportune time. Mrs. Charles and I are expecting our first-born (a son, of course!) early next month, and, as you know, cigars are so darned expensive these days!

Again, my sincerest thanks.

Cordially,

Incoming letter

Dear Sally,

I'm sending this little package via my husband this morning, in the hope that it is something which will help make your Christmas a merry one.

We both wish you all the joys of the holiday season.

Cordially,

Answering letter

For a Christmas Gift—Business

Dear Mrs. Crowley,

When your husband laid a package on my desk the day before Christmas and said that it was a "little remembrance" from you, I must admit I had to force myself to wait until Christmas morning to open it.

How can I ever thank you, Mrs. Crowley! Such a glamorous gift, and in your usual excellent good taste! I don't know when anything has given me such delight.

I hope the New Year will be happy and prosperous for you and your family. The fact that you thought of me in such a friendly fashion, with such a warm and attractive gift, will get my own New Year off to the very best possible start.

Sincerely,

IX

Letters OF REMINDER

AND FOLLOW-UP

♣ When a business matter or appointment is extremely important, the good secretary can avoid last-minute delays, cancellations and lost time by paying particular attention to the reminder letter. Sometimes a simple reminder note is used only to reaffirm plans. Often it is used to seek confirmation of a date and frequently it activates the recipient to fulfill a promise made (and perhaps forgotten). As in most business letters, the reminder correspondence should be specific rather than general.

CHECK LIST
FOR LETTERS OF REMINDER AND FOLLOW-UP

1. Refer to the initial time when the date of commitment was made.
2. Offer the reminder or follow-up as a routine matter and *not* because you think the recipient is absent-minded or forgetful.

3. Spell out again the time, place, date, etc.

4. Ask for confirmation where feasible.

Incoming letter

Business Luncheon

Dear Larry,

This is just a reminder that we've reserved a table for ten at the Waldorf for Wednesday noon, January 10th. This is for luncheon during the Eastern Sales Managers' semi-annual meeting, you'll recall. You've promised to fill seven seats at the table with your own salesmen. Since we made the date some time ago, I thought this little reminder might be fitting.

When you get a chance, and before January 4th, will you send me the names of the salesmen who'll attend?

Cordially,

Answering letter

Dear Bill,

Thanks for the reminder about the meeting on Wednesday, January 10th. We are still planning to occupy the seven seats you have reserved for us at the luncheon. My secretary is rounding up the boys to confirm this date and she will send the names along to you well ahead of January 4th.

Cordially,

Incoming letter

Desire to See New Merchandise

Dear Mr. Hewitt,

Last spring, when I was thinking about a new car, you suggested that I wait until fall when the new lines would arrive. So far, I've heard nothing from you and it seems to me that you should have something for me to look at very soon. Will you let me know right away, Mr. Hewitt?

Cordially,

Answering letter

Dear Mr. Dixon,

I've just received my first shipment of Buick Specials and I know you'll want to come in and look at them as well as take one out for a trial run.

This year's Buicks have a number of new features which I think will interest you. I can deliver to you a four-door sedan, with radio, heater, power steering and power brakes, white-wall tires and wheel covers, for under $3,200. Of course, there will be an allowance on your old car, too, if you wish to use it as a trade-in.

We're open Thursday and Friday evenings. Why not stop in after work and have a chat? I think you'll be as excited as I am at the new Buick Special line.

Cordially,

Incoming letter

Follow-Up on Sales Promotion

Dear Mr. Brown,

Last September, I demonstrated to you and your associates the new packaging methods we had devised with your company in mind. Since your budget for the fiscal year was nearly exhausted at that time, you suggested that I contact you again in about six months.

Now, Mr. Brown, we are well into 1965 and I know your new fiscal year starts in July. I'm still confident that the suggested packaging can save you a great deal of money, so perhaps you'll want me to come in to see you within the next week or two, so that you can have exact figures when you start budgeting for the fiscal year ahead.

Will you have your secretary phone me at Wilson 5-1244 any morning before 11 o'clock? I'll be happy to come in any afternoon you suggest.

Cordially,

Answering letter

Dear Mr. Jarvis,

Mr. Brown will be very glad to see you and discuss with you the new packaging methods you have for our company. He and Mr. Herbit will expect you on Tuesday, April the 12th, at 2 o'clock.

Cordially,

Incoming letter

Follow-up on Sales Promotion

Dear Mr. Smith,

On April 25th, I wrote you about our new shipment of transistors, telling you of the special discounts that were available only through the month of May. I'm sure you realize that these prices cannot be matched anywhere else.

This is just to remind you that the price quoted to you in my previous letter will not hold after May 30th. Since today is the 20th of the month, I'm sure you'll want to place your order at once. Additional quantity discounts also apply, so this is truly a once-in-a-lifetime opportunity.

Why don't you send me your order by return mail?

Cordially,

Answering letter

Dear Mr. Logan,

Please ship 250 transistors at the special discount you quoted me on April 25th.

Thank you very much for reminding me again so that I am able to take advantage of this special offer.

Cordially,

Incoming letter

Conducting a Seminar

Dear Mr. Goldman,

My secretary brought in my follow-up file this morning and on the top of the pile was my letter to you dated August 17th. Since I've not received an answer, it occurs to me that, through some peculiar circumstance, my letter may have gone astray. If so, you'll find a carbon copy enclosed. On the other hand, I realize that the pressure of business may have prevented your answering the letter if you've received it.

Either way, I'd most certainly like an early expression from you in connection with my suggestion that you conduct a new-products seminar at our fall meeting. Will you drop me a line at your earliest convenience so that I may proceed with my plans? And I *do* hope you'll see fit to take on the project.

Cordially,

Answering letter

Dear Mr. Thomas,

I'm sorry about the delay in answering your letter of August 17th, and I hasten to assure you that I will be happy to conduct the seminar on new products at the fall meeting. Thank you very much for asking me. I'm looking forward to the meeting and especially because I will be seeing so many of my old friends in your area.

Cordially,

Incoming letter

Invitation to Seminar—Reminder

Dear Mrs. Whitman,

I haven't heard from you since our chat a few weeks ago about the possibility of your attendance at the Better Business Seminar to be conducted at Arden House in New York for the three days starting August 14th.

If you're still interested, and I hope you are, I'll need your commitment at once. We can only accommodate 75 people and the reservations are coming in fast.

I'm sure that, like most of those who've attended these seminars in the past, you'll come away with a dozen or more ideas for furthering the efficiency of the department which you operate.

Please let me hear from you by return mail.

Cordially,

Answering letter

Dear Mrs. Ruthel,

Thank you very much for reminding me about the Better Business Seminar. I am glad to report that I will be able to attend the meeting each day for three days starting August 14th.

It will be a pleasure to see you again and I am certain that, as you say, I'll return with many good ideas about promoting greater efficiency on the job here at Excelsior.

Cordially,

Incoming letter

Date of Committee Meeting

Dear Boss,

This is just a reminder that you have a committee meeting scheduled for Wednesday afternoon, the 30th, here at the office. Since your return date from Chicago was uncertain when you wrote on Monday, I thought I'd better call this to your attention.

Everyone has been notified about the meeting so, if the date still holds, nothing more need be done. But if you can't get back in time for it, you'd better let me know an alternative date and I'll notify all of those concerned.

Sincerely,

Answering letter

Dear Alice,

Thanks for reminding me again about the meeting which I had scheduled for Wednesday afternoon. Right now it looks as if I will be delayed in returning from Chicago—so will you please phone all the men and ask them to come instead on Friday, September 1st, at 2:00 P.M.?

Cordially,

X

Letters OF RECOMMENDATION

❦ Unless one can be completely honest in writing a letter of recommendation, it is better to avoid writing one. Such letters reflect not only on the character and ability of the person recommended, but, in a less direct fashion, on the judgment, character and ability of the person who writes the letter. This means that, usually, you will not want to write a letter of reference or recommendation unless you, or your employer, is actually in a position to do so. Either the person must be known to you rather well on a social or business basis, or his or her accomplishments are so widely acclaimed that there can be no doubt about them.

On the rare occasion when a letter of recommendation is required of you after only slight acquaintance with the person to be recommended, it is important that you qualify your recommendation within the bounds of your knowledge of the person and his ability.

CHECK LIST
FOR LETTERS OF RECOMMENDATION

1. Be truthful but temper your comments with humanity.
2. Don't let personal animosity affect your judgment of a person's ability.
3. Admit freely that employees relate differently to different employers.

Incoming letter

Dear Mr. Burns,

Miss Mary Severno has just applied for a position with this company as secretary to one of our vice-presidents. She has given us your name as a former employer and we'd appreciate it very much, therefore, if you would write us giving your opinion of her ability.

Cordially,

Answering letter

Personal Secretary

Dear Mrs. Kramer,

It's a pleasure to write a letter of recommendation on behalf of Miss Mary Severno. She was employed by this organization as my personal secretary from 1951 through November 1958. She left for family reasons, and now she is again looking for employment. I'd like it very much indeed if there were an opening here so that we could have her back with us again. However, there are no openings at the present time.

We found Miss Severno to be a young lady of high integrity, who worked tirelessly and most efficiently. Her tact is unquestionable, her secretarial abilities topnotch. She was a valued employee from every point of view.

Cordially,

Incoming letter

Dear Mr. Dwyer,

When I left your employ two months ago, I forgot to ask you for a letter of recommendation. Now, I am being considered for a job with a well-known law firm in San Francisco and I wonder if you'd be kind enough to give me such a letter. My prospective employer has asked for details about my responsibilities with Benton & Dwyer, so I'd appreciate it if you can give him some indication of the duties which were mine.

Will you send your letter of recommendation directly to Mr. Wadsworth Adams at Adams & Niece, 22 Park Place, San Francisco, California?

Thanks very much for your help.

Sincerely,

Answering letter

Personal Secretary

Dear Mr. Adams,

At the request of Miss Margaret Merkel, a former employee of ours, I am writing this letter.

Miss Merkel was with us for three years, acting as my personal secretary. In addition, she handled many details which are normally assigned to an office manager. She is extremely personable, a quick and accurate stenographer and typist. Her attendance record was excellent, too, so I believe she will prove to be a most capable and dependable employee.

Cordially,

Incoming letter

Dear Mrs. Hammacher,

A young lady by the name of Miss Joan Hall has sent in her application for a clerical position in our statistical department. We will have her come in next week for a personal interview. In the meantime, will you be kind enough to give us information (in confidence) about her qualifications? She wrote your name on the application as her former employer.

Thank you very much.

Cordially,

Answering letter

Secretarial or Clerical Position

Dear Mrs. Kramer,

Miss Joan Hall was with us only a few weeks and she left our employ before we had an opportunity to know her well. She seemed a very pleasant young lady who made an excellent appearance. Her schooling and previous job background should have prepared her well for a secretarial position, so perhaps it was the unique character of our work— or a temporary personal problem—which prevented her from filling the bill here.

Sincerely,

Incoming letter

Dear Mr. Cutter,

Now that little John has finished grade school and gone off to Andover Prep, I find that I need something to do in order to use up my spare time. Next week I will go job hunting.

Will you be kind enough to send me an open letter of reference? It would help me a great deal, I know. Thanks very much.

Cordially,

Answering letter

Open Letter of Recommendation
Executive Secretary

TO WHOM IT MAY CONCERN:

Mrs. Martha Stevens was employed as my personal secretary from early 1952 through November, 1957. During that time, she proved to be a remarkable young woman who combined all the qualities necessary to make her a topnotch executive secretary.

She worked tirelessly and efficiently during the years she was with us, and I found her completely trustworthy in every respect.

I'm happy to recommend her and shall be pleased to supply further information should it be required.

Cordially,

Incoming letter

Dear Mr. Samuelson,

Even though my stay with you in the Statistical Department was of short duration, I wonder if you would supply me with an open letter of reference.

I'm still looking for the position where I can use my knowledge of cost and time study methods in tax situations, and feel that some expression of my capability from you will be extremely helpful in my interviews.

Thanks very much.

Cordially,

Answering letter

Open Letter of Recommendation
Statistical Position

TO WHOM IT MAY CONCERN:

Every once in a while, an employee comes along who is too skilled for the job at hand. This is true in the case of Henry R. Johnston, the bearer of this letter.

Mr. Johnston applied to us when we had a clerical opening in our Statistical Department last June. We hired him but it didn't take us long to learn that his abilities were far in excess of the demands of the job assigned him. Had we not already been satisfied with our Statistical Chief, Mr. Johnston would most certainly have been offered that position. However, at the present time we have no position which is suitable, so we and Mr. Johnston have regrettably parted company.

I can recommend Mr. Johnston unqualifiedly for any position requiring superior ability with figures, knowledge of cost and time study methods and matters to do with taxes. He is a responsible, conscientious employee.

Very truly yours,

Incoming letter

Dear Mr. Stark,

I understand that Mr. Frank Munson was employed by you from April 1960 to January 1961, in the capacity of sales manager.

Mr. Munson has applied to us for a similar position and has given your name as reference. Will you be kind enough to give me a case history about Mr. Munson, touching on his ability, his initiative and willingness to take responsibility and also why, if you can reveal it, the reason for his termination?

Mr. Munson also mentioned a physical handicap which he states was not a business handicap in the position he held with you. Can you elaborate on this subject, please?

Naturally, any information you give will be held in the strictest confidence. Frankly, I like many things about Mr. Munson, but his short term of employment in most previous jobs has me worried.

Cordially,

Answering letter

Salesmanship—Physical Handicap

Dear Mr. Eldridge,

Let me assure you. Mr. Frank Munson was a reliable and valuable employee. His physical problem had no effect on his business activities, and we were, indeed, sorry to terminate his employment.

However, under a new policy instituted last fall, we eliminated the position of midwestern sales manager in favor of a part-time representative. Since Mr. Munson wanted and required a full-time position, he refused to take on this part-time representation. We had no other positions for which he was qualified at that time.

I repeat that we were sorry to see him go. He is a very able and hard-working salesman, well qualified to manage a sales team.

Cordially,

Incoming letter

Dear Mr. Southergill,

Yesterday, a young man by the name of John Sykes came in to apply for the position of sales manager. He seemed to have a good grasp of all the fundamentals required in this position. However, I can't help but feel that the physical handicap from which he suffers may make it difficult for him to hold up under the pressure.

I'll be grateful to you for your frank opinion about this, Mr. Southergill.

Cordially,

Answering letter

Sales Manager—Physical Handicap

Dear Mr. Eldridge,

I shall be perfectly frank with you. Mr. John Sykes is a very likeable and personable gentleman. But I think his physical problems make a sales manager's position a little too strenuous for him, though I can understand why he is loath to acknowledge this.

After working with him for some months, it strikes me that his proper groove would be somewhere in the field of promotion rather than sales, since this should not normally require so much of him physically in the way of out of town trips, etc.

Perhaps the activity in the sales divisions of our company is somewhat unique, and in an organization where the pressure from travel is not quite so heavy, Mr. Sykes might fill the bill. There is certainly no doubt of the fact that he likes and understands sales and sales management.

Cordially,

Incoming letter

Dear Mr. Leafgreen,

The New Mexico Chamber of Commerce is preparing a 1965 brochure to promote travel in this glorious state. Your name was given to me by the manager of the Hotel Rancho Grande because he said your enthusiasm for New Mexico was so beautifully expressed after your recent visit.

We'd like so much to have a letter from you for publication in the new brochure, if you would see fit to write one giving your impressions of this area.

I hope you'll comply with this request and that you'll accept the little token of advance appreciation I'm sending under separate cover.

Cordially,

Answering letter

Travel Promotion

Dear Mr. Smith,

For years, I've dreamed of visiting New Mexico and the dream came true about two months ago when my wife and I toured the entire west and near-west country, ending our trip with a two week's stay in Santa Fe.

I want to compliment you on the splendid job being done by the New Mexico Chamber of Commerce. Personnel at the various information booths were both courteous and helpful. The hotels and motels recommended were ideal. The roads and routing signs throughout the state made our tour delightful and without frustration.

You may use this letter when you promote your services, if you wish. It isn't often I feel so strongly that I take pen in hand.

Sincerely,

Incoming letter

Expert Accounting

Dear Mr. Parkhill,

I don't know whether you recall this, but about two weeks ago when we played at your table during a duplicate tournament at the club, you asked if I could recommend an accountant who was well qualified to handle tax matters for you.

I'd like to suggest that you contact Mr. William Stephens, 23 Sound Drive, Port Washington. Mr. Stephens is a certified public accountant who has been preparing both my personal and business tax returns for four or five years. I have been very well satisfied with his work, and since the Internal Revenue Service has never questioned my tax returns, I am reasonably sure that he knows his stuff.

You may use my name, if you choose, when contacting him.

Cordially,

Answering letter

Dear Mr. Coons,

I remember well our discussion of accountants when we met at the club, and I want to thank you for recommending Mr. Stephens.

Since that day, my associate here at the office has gone over the books with me and after some discussion we find that our problem is not so great as we had anticipated. Therefore, I'll not call on Mr. Stephens this year, but I will surely keep him in mind if something comes up in the future where we will need the services of an accountant and tax expert.

Cordially,

Incoming letter

Dear Mr. Sanderson,

We're embarking on a small campaign by mail to interest new customers in our packaging service. Since we have been handling your shipping problems for the last three years, I think a letter of recommendation from you in our behalf would be most effective in helping to achieve our goal. Will you give us such a letter, Mr. Sanderson? It would certainly be appreciated.

Cordially,

Answering letter

A Service

Dear Mr. Jones,

I'd like to tell you how very pleased we are with your service. It has enabled us to cut down materially on office help and at the same time expedite delivery to our customers.

I'll be happy to recommend your service to anyone who cares to inquire and you may use this letter as you see fit, if it will help you with prospective clients.

Cordially,

Incoming letter

Dear Mr. Stone,

We are seriously considering the practicality of signing up with Hotel Services, Incorporated, for their housecleaning and chambermaid services. Your name has been given to us as a reference and we're told that you have been using these services for several years.

Will you be good enough to tell me candidly how you feel about this type of service? I assume that you are pleased with it, for you continue to use it, but on the other hand, I know that sometimes a contract necessitates staying with something that doesn't please us too well.

Any information you can give me will be much appreciated and held, of course, in the strictest confidence.

Cordially,

Answering letter

Unsatisfactory Service

Dear Mr. Morton,

You must have a crystal ball! We have been very much disappointed with the services we contracted for with Hotel Services and shall not renew this arrangement when our present contract expires, which I believe is next June.

These people started out like a house afire. They cleaned our hotel rooms beautifully and promptly. Their maid service in the beginning was excellent, too. But alas! this must have been a case of the "new broom." We have had to hire an auxiliary staff for the past six months, simply to amplify and improve upon the quality of the work now being performed by Hotel Services.

I am now thoroughly convinced that no such outside contractor can supply, over the long term, the kind of personalized service a good hotel needs to offer its clientele.

I hope this information will prove helpful.

Cordially,

XI

Letters ON TRIP PLANNING

When a secretary is entrusted with the planning of her employer's itinerary, whether for a short or a lengthy trip, within the country or abroad, she must go to every possible length to avoid mistakes of any kind. No employer can be happy to find upon arrival at an airport that his secretary has made a mistake and written down the wrong time for his departure. No employer can smile merrily when he discovers upon inquiry at the hotel reservation desk that he has no room reservation.

Thus, to insure not only accuracy but the fulfillment of her employer's wishes about his business travels, the good secretary starts out with a tentative itinerary, after having made tentative reservations which must later be confirmed.

When the tentative itinerary is complete, the secretary turns it over to her employer for his approval. Once this is secured, she immediately puts into writing confirmation of all the reservations she has previously made.

For double security, she makes every possible effort to get written confirmation from those with whom she has made these reservations. These letters or cards of confirmation are turned over to her employer before his departure, so that he may use them as evidence of his reservations should any confusion arise.

Securing travel information and then making travel reservations are part of the good secretary's responsibilities. Most frequently she deals with a travel agency by telephone and sometimes she seeks preliminary information by letter. She always tries to end up with verified reservations in writing.

CHECK LIST

FOR TRIP PLANNING

1. Work with travel agent wherever possible.
2. Suggest alternate routes and hotels where doubt exists about securing first choice.
3. Ask for *written* confirmation of all reservations.

Incoming letter

Making Hotel Reservations

Gentlemen,

Please reserve for Mr. Howard H. Wilkinson a moderately priced single room with bath for April 11th to April 14th. Mr. Wilkinson plans to arrive about noon on Thursday April 11th. Will you please confirm this reservation and indicate what the rate will be?

Yours very truly,

Answering letter

Dear Mr. Wilkinson,

We have reserved a single room with bath for Mr. Wilkinson for April 11th through April 14th.

The rate for this room will be $15 per day.

Cordially,

Incoming letter

Changing Dates of Reservations

Dear Sir,

Several weeks ago, I reserved adjoining rooms and bath for my employer, Mr. Charles Wilson, and our sales manager, Mr. William Cathcart, for the nights of March 10th and 11th.

These gentlemen will not be able to make the trip to Houston on those dates, but instead will be there on the 14th and 15th of March. Will you please reserve the same accommodations for them and send me a written confirmation of this change?

Thank you very much.

Cordially,

Answering letter

Dear Miss Wilson,

We have cancelled the reservations for adjoining rooms and bath for Mr. Charles Wilson and Mr. William Cathcart for March 10th and March 11th, and have reserved the same

accommodations for the 14th and 15th, as you requested in
your letter of March 3rd.

Sincerely,

Incoming letter

Group Accommodations

Gentlemen,

Will you please send me by return mail the rates for a
penthouse suite with two twin-bed rooms and a parlor to
accommodate four of our salesmen from Friday, July 2nd,
through the night of Wednesday, July 7th?

If a penthouse suite will not be available for those dates,
please send rates for other suites which will comfortably accommodate this same number.

I'd appreciate your prompt reply, since I must complete
reservations before the end of next week.

Cordially,

Answering letter

Dear Mr. McGinnis,

We are very sorry but all penthouse suites have been
reserved from July 2nd through July 7th.

However, we have a deluxe suite consisting of a parlor
and two twin-bed rooms on the 10th floor overlooking the
park, which we think would be suitable for your salesmen
on the dates requested.

We have reserved this suite for you since the time is
growing short. The cost will be $55 per night. Will you
please let us know by return mail if this is satisfactory?

Cordially,

Incoming letter

Hotels Abroad

Gentlemen,

Mr. Henry Nelson, President of this company, will leave New York on the Queen Mary on February 23rd. You have already confirmed his reservations.

Upon arrival in Southampton, Mr. Nelson is a little uncertain of his forthcoming itinerary. He will probably need to visit Antwerp, Geneva, Rome, Paris and finally London.

Because of the indefinite aspects of this itinerary, will you be kind enough to send me the name of a suitable hotel in each of those cities, with rates, if possible? Mr. Nelson will probably have to make his own reservations after arrival in Southampton.

Cordially,

Answering letter

Dear Miss Sweet,

We are enclosing lists of deluxe and first class hotels in Antwerp, Geneva, Rome, Paris and London, with check marks after each hotel which we believe will meet with Mr. Nelson's requirements. The rates are also shown on the lists.

Before Mr. Nelson leaves each city he should have the concierge make a reservation for him at his next stop. This will assure him of a definite and satisfactory reservation in each city, which is especially important during the summer season.

If there is any other way we can be of help in making Mr. Nelson's trip a pleasant one please do not hesitate to call on us.

Cordially,

Incoming letter

Routing via Airlines

Gentlemen,

Can you help me promptly, please, in routing my employer, Mr. John Emerson, from New York by American to Seattle, Washington, and include stopovers in the following cities?

Pittsburgh	a full day
Cleveland	one afternoon
Cincinnati	one morning
Louisville	two or three hours
Minneapolis	a day and a night

Mr. Emerson hopes to depart from New York early on the morning of January 9th and must be in Seattle no later than noon on January 13th. He wants to remain in Seattle through January 20th and then wishes a direct flight back to Newark, if possible.

Thank you for your attention and assistance.

Cordially,

Answering letter

Dear Miss Terryton,

We can offer the following schedule in order to help Mr. Emerson complete his arrangements for the trip from New York to Seattle, with stopovers:

	Arrive	*Date*	*Depart*	*Date*
New York			6:30 AM	1/9/64
Pittsburgh	8:14 AM	1/9/64	10:00 AM	1/10/64
Cleveland	11:30 AM	1/10/64	6:00 PM	1/10/64
Cincinnati	7:00 PM	1/10/64	1:00 PM	1/11/64

	Arrive	Date	Depart	Date
Louisville	2:00 PM	1/11/64	8:00 PM	1/11/64
Minneapolis	10:15 PM	1/11/64	8:00 AM	1/13/64
Seattle	9:00 AM	1/13/64	8:15 AM	1/21/64
Newark	2:30 PM	1/21/64		

The time indicated in each city is local time. If this schedule is satisfactory for Mr. Emerson, please let us know as quickly as possible so that we can make reservations accordingly.

Cordially,

Incoming letter

Cruise Literature

Gentlemen,

My employer, Mr. Davis Emerson, and his wife are planning a Caribbean cruise for mid-February. They are anxious to spend a little time at each of the following ports: Panama, Nassau, Bermuda, Jamaica and the Virgin Islands. They cannot be gone more than 28 days.

Will you be kind enough to send to my attention literature in connection with several cruises and ships which will visit those ports or most of them, leaving New York no earlier than February 10th? I would also appreciate complete details about stopovers, costs and stateroom availabilities in both first class and cabin class.

Very truly yours,

Answering letter

Dear Miss Angle,

We are enclosing literature giving ports of call, rates and general information on sailings to the Caribbean in mid-

February. There are two ships which we could recommend highly for Mr. and Mrs. Emerson. They are the *Baltic* and the *Star* of the Whitehall Line, each carrying 150 passengers.

We're sure Mr. and Mrs. Emerson will find all the answers to their questions in the booklet "How to Enjoy Four Weeks on a Small Ship." If they require additional information, please let us hear from you.

Very truly yours,

Incoming letter

Bon Voyage Luncheon

Gentlemen,

I wish to entertain at luncheon at *Voisin's* on Monday, April third, around 1:00 P.M. This will be a bon voyage party for two members of our firm who are starting on a trip around the world.

There will be 20 people at the luncheon so, if possible, I'd prefer a private dining room. We'd like the services of your wine steward and will choose our luncheons from your menu.

Will you please acknowledge this reservation by return mail?

Cordially,

Answering letter

Dear Mr. Boise,

This will confirm your reservation for a private dining room for a bon voyage party on Monday, April 3rd, at one o'clock.

We can offer you the Green Room, seating 20 people

at one oval shaped table, with the services of a wine steward, at $5 per person. Your guests may choose their luncheons from our regular à la carte menu.

Will you let us know by April 1st if this arrangement meets with your approval?

Cordially,

Incoming letter

Convention Banquet

Dear Sir,

This organization has completed plans with the resident manager to hold its 20th annual convention at the Waldorf Astoria the week of April 1st. I wish to arrange for a banquet on the evening of April 2nd and, at this time, it's impossible for me to tell you how many will attend.

Normally, there are about 200 who attend these conventions, so for the moment, will you estimate for me what it will cost to serve a first-class dinner in the Starlight Dining Room for 200 guests? Your price should include two cocktails per person. I'd like you to also send me several menu suggestions so that I may make a choice of what shall be served.

Time is really getting short and I need to notify convention members of our arrangements. I hope you can give this, therefore, your prompt attention.

Cordially,

Answering letter

Dear Mr. Manning,

We will be very pleased to arrange a banquet on Thursday evening, April 2nd, for the 20th annual convention of your organization. Based on approximately 200 guests in the

Starlight Dining Room, we can serve you our finest cuisine, preceded by two cocktails per person, for only $3.75 per person.

We are enclosing several sample menus which are currently popular and which we can recommend highly. Will you please let us know within the next few days, if you wish to make this a definite reservation? Then we can complete the details of the menu and make any other necessary arrangements. We will need to know the exact number of dinner guests by March 20th.

Cordially,

XII

Letters OF SYMPATHY

❦ There are few letters more difficult to write than the letter of sympathy or condolence. Yet such letters must be written and they are usually more appreciated than any other correspondence in the world of business.

A good rule to remember is that the letter of sympathy may be extremely brief, provided it conveys a sincere and heartfelt expression of warmth and understanding.

Don't try to flavor your letter of condolence with religious or sentimental undertones unless you are positive the recipient holds the same viewpoint as your own. Try not to add to the recipient's grief by dwelling at length on the sorrow or tragedy which has befallen him. On the other hand, it's not necessary to mince words to the point of completely ignoring the reason for your letter.

CHECK LIST
FOR LETTERS OF SYMPATHY

1. Keep it brief.
2. Don't be macabre!
3. Don't tell about your own troubles.
4. Offer assistance only where such assistance is realistic.
5. Don't be flowery or sentimental.

Incoming letter

Dear Mr. Henry,

I'm sure that you met Mr. William Hartstone at the last convention of the Harkness Company, and that you have done some business with him since that time. Now, it is my sad duty to tell you that Mr. Hartstone passed away quietly in his sleep last night. Even though Mrs. Hartstone is holding up bravely, it would be thoughtful of you to drop her a line.

Cordially,

Answering letter

To Widow of Business Associate

Dear Mrs. Hartstone,

Mrs. Henry joins me in expressing my sadness at the untimely death of your husband.

We did not know Mr. Hartstone very long, but in the short time it was our privilege to enjoy his friendship, we found him a delightful and personable gentleman, whose first thought seemed always to be "What can I do to help you?"

Perhaps the knowledge that our thoughts are with you at this time will help just a little bit to sustain you.

Sincerely,

Incoming letter

Dear Ben,

   It came as a tremendous shock to me that Mr. Ernest Blenham, President of Pioneer, passed away two days ago. I thought I should write you right away because you may not have read the newspaper item mentioning his death. You may want to send some word of sympathy to your friend there, Vernon Garner.

Cordially,

Answering letter

Loss of Company Official

Dear Vernon,

   I know how much you and everyone else at Pioneer liked and respected Mr. Blenham. His death is most certainly a serious loss from a personal as well as business standpoint.
   Please convey to the rest of your staff my sincere sympathy.

Very truly yours,

Incoming letter

Dear Harry,

   Just in case you didn't see yesterday's *Herald*—Edward Muller passed away on Wednesday following his long illness. I'm writing you, for I know how much you enjoyed working with him and that you may want to get a note off to Mrs. Muller.

Cordially,

Answering letter

Business Associate

Dear Mrs. Muller,

I was shocked and distressed to learn of Edward's passing. As you know, we were business associates for many years and had become fast friends, as well, since Edward joined Morrow & Company. If there is anything at all I can do to help you at this sorrowful time, please pick up the phone and tell me so. I shall miss Edward very much.

Cordially,

Incoming letter

Dear Mr. Schrader,

Just after Mr. Fellow left your office Tuesday, his car skidded and went into a spin. Mr. Fellow suffered a broken rib and some bruises. His car was badly damaged, to boot. He is at the Simsbury Hospital and would appreciate a note from you, I'm sure.

He's been wondering if this delay in filling out the forms and returning them to your office will in any way affect his new insurance policy.

Cordially,

Answering letter

An Accident and Injuries

Dear Mr. Fellow,

Your secretary just wrote me of your distressing accident and I am relieved to learn that though your injuries are painful, they are less serious than they might have been and that you are recovering speedily.

I just want you to know that there is no need at all to be in a hurry to fill out the necessary insurance forms. When you are feeling better, I'll stop by and together we can fill out the forms very quickly. I'm so glad that you are as well covered as you are, for that means at least that you won't have any expense in connection with the repairs to your car.

Do let me know if there is anything I can do while you are laid up.

Sincerely,

Incoming letter

Dear Jed,

Did you hear over the radio this morning that Harry Cobleigh was in a rather bad auto crash just after he left home for work yesterday morning?

He is still in the Maplewood Hospital. His condition is not serious but his injuries are quite painful—a broken leg and arm. I know you will want to get a note off to him.

Cordially,

Answering letter

An Accident and Injuries

Dear Mr. Cobleigh,

I was sorry to learn of your accident from Ned Dobbs, but I'm glad to know that while your injuries are painful, they are not dangerous. While you are recuperating, perhaps the novel I'm sending with this note will help you pass the time.

If there's anything at all I can do to help you or your family during your convalescence, be sure to let me know.

Sincerely,

Incoming letter

Dear Imogene,

I don't know whether you've heard the latest news about Frank's illness. The surgery was not too successful, which means that Frank is in for a longer period of convalescence and only time will tell the results.

Knowing how fond you are of both Mary and Frank, anything you can do to cheer up either or both of them will be greatly appreciated.

Cordially,

Answering letter

Serious Illness

Dear Mary,

Your sister wrote me about Frank's illness and I want you to know that I'm extremely sorry the recent surgery was not more successful.

Marjorie tells me that the most important thing right now is to keep Frank comfortable and free from worry. Please pick up the phone and call me if there is anything at all that I can do to help you accomplish that.

Perhaps a little later on, the doctor may permit callers. If so, and you think a brief visit from me will bring Frank a little cheer, just let me know. And give Frank my very fondest good wishes, please.

Sincerely,

Incoming letter

Dear Allan,

The Foster Machines Company lost one of its huge warehouses in a fire last Monday. Knowing that you are not too far away, and that you have done business with Mr. Foster over these many years—I think they are in need of space for some of the material which was removed before the building collapsed. Can you help out, Allan?

Cordially,

Answering letter

Loss by Fire—Offer of Assistance

Dear Mr. Foster,

Is there anything at all that we at Simsbury & Company can do to help you in this most difficult time? Some years ago, we suffered a similar loss when our warehouse was totally destroyed by fire. It was only through the assistance of our good friends that we were able to function reasonably well during the three months it took to rebuild.

Please let me know how we can be of service. Perhaps we can help you by letting you use one of our warehouses for a while. Just call me at Exeter 6-1300.

Cordially,

Incoming letter

Loss of Home by Fire

Dear Catherine,

I want you to know how sorry I was to learn of the fire which destroyed your home last week. I am sure you are comforted by the fact that neither you nor your mother were injured in any way but, on the other hand, it must surely trouble you to have lost the accumulations of a lifetime; no amount of insurance can replace the things one loved for sentimental reasons.

I remember how much you liked the little music box I brought back to you from Switzerland last year. Perhaps the fact that the package which accompanies this note contains an identical one will help to cheer you just a little.

Please let me know if there is anything at all I can do to make things easier or to make you or your mother comfortable.

Sincerely,

Answering letter

Dear Margie,

How kind and thoughtful of you to send the music box just when it seems that the bottom has dropped out of everything! Mother and I are so grateful that we got out of the house before it collapsed, and as sad as we are over losing our lovely home and belongings—we are also grateful for our kind friends who are helping in so many endearing ways.

Thank you so very much for remembering. . . .

Affectionately,

XIII

Sales LETTERS

A sales letter is a sales call in writing. Before a good sales letter can be written, therefore, the writer must know his company and its product thoroughly, must recognize the advantages and disadvantages (if any) of those products, must know what competitive products are available. Most important of all, the writer of a sales letter must *believe* in the products or services he is trying to sell.

Once this background of knowledge is established, the writer of a sales letter must acquaint himself with the power of persuasion, because every sales letter, like every personal call, must offer persuasive and salient reasons why the customer cannot do without the products or services offered. Sometimes there are a dozen or more such points to be made but often the whole picture can be condensed to a single persuasive tool which could be price, quality, versatility of uses, etc. This means that one must understand the problems and aims of the customer, too.

When the necessary understanding of sales goals and attributes is achieved, it then pays to study well-written sales letters, of which there are many kinds.

Sometimes an extra measure of impact can be inculcated in a business letter by the use of what is often known as the *gimmick*. (Gimmick seems to be a modern and somewhat slangy replacement for the Victorian expression "gimcrack," which is defined in the dictionary as "a showy, useless trifle; a trivial knicknack.")

Often, in correspondence, this gimmick can truly be a trivial article which ties in cleverly or memorably with the letter, itself. Then again, the gimmick might only be a device within the letter which encourages the recipient to take quick, almost immediate action, the right kind of action.

When thinking of this type of letter, it's important to keep in mind that the gimmick itself must not be the reason for the letter. It must simply be an imaginative and appropriate adjunct. A few illustrative letters of this type are shown, too, along with the more traditional and conservative type of sales letter.

CHECK LIST

FOR SALES LETTERS

1. Describe your product or service.
2. Explain how it fits into your prospect's over-all situation.
3. Offer to demonstrate, where possible.
4. Leave one unexplained point or unanswered question, for further contact.
5. Create a desire to know more about the product or to see it in action.

Incoming letter

Advertising Sales Letter

high fidelity • THE PUBLISHING HOUSE • GREAT BARRINGTON • MASS.
THE MAGAZINE FOR MUSIC LISTENERS

                                                    August 1, 1961,

Dear Sir:

    The other day I sent my son Chris to the delicatessen for a half pint of cream. Boylike, he must have had other more weighty matters on his mind because he showed up, eventually, with a quart of milk.

    While he was on his way back to the store, I couldn't help but reflect that a similar mistake is sometimes made by advertisers in the home music listening market: they want <u>cream</u>, but they end up with <u>milk</u>.

    For example, do each of the magazines on your schedule reach the maximum number of logical prospects for your product? Or are the returns from your advertising dollars diluted by a sizable proportion of readers who have little or no interest in music?

    In other words, are you buying "cream" --- or "milk?"

    In any selection of media arrived at with these important considerations in mind, HIGH FIDELITY will almost certainly rate as your number one choice.

    HIGH FIDELITY, as you know, is strictly a magazine for music listeners. This is its sole reason for being. Its entire editorial content is designed to appeal to discriminating people who enjoy listening to music in their homes.

    That such an audience would naturally be attracted to a magazine of its type goes almost without saying. But we make sure of this by directing our subscription promotion accordingly -- with the accent on <u>quality</u> instead of <u>quantity</u>. No questionable "gimmicks" here to boost circulation overnight! Just a steady, sustained effort aimed at the discerning and the sophisticated among music listeners -- the kind of people who, when they do become subscribers to HIGH FIDELITY, are automatically excellent prospects for the products and services of our advertisers.

    HIGH FIDELITY'S ABC statement for the six month period ended June 30, 1961 shows net paid average of 110,481 -- up from the previous six month's average of 106,076. You can buy more numbers, of course. But you won't find another magazine in the entire field that will equal HIGH FIDELITY'S return on your advertising investment. And you don't need to take my unsupported word for this. <u>Advertisers' own carefully kept records show that HIGH FIDELITY consistently outpulls its competition when results are figured on a per-dollar-invested basis.</u>

    The reason? HIGH FIDELITY delivers the cream -- not the milk!

                                    Cordially,

                                    Claire N. Eddings

                                    (Mrs.) Claire N. Eddings
                                    Director of Advertising Sales

Answering letter

Dear Mrs. Eddings,

We enjoyed reading your August 1st letter. We agree with you—numbers are not half so important as quality. Keep skimming off the cream. That's what we want!

Cordially,

Incoming letter

Dear Mr. Jensen,

After considerable thought, we have decided not to purchase your duplicating machine at this time. Quite frankly, after experimentation with it, we find that it is somewhat overpriced and believe we can get equivalent, or perhaps even better, performance for several hundred dollars less.

Will you, therefore, arrange to have someone from your organization pick up the machine at your earliest convenience? Thanks very much for letting us try it.

Cordially,

Answering letter

After Rejection of Merchandise

Dear Mr. Russo,

I will pick up our duplicating machine on my next trip to DuKane, which should be either Thursday or Friday of next week.

In your letter, you mentioned that you thought the Model 100-AS was overpriced and that you thought you could do as well or better for several hundred dollars less. Perhaps this is so, but I know of no other machine on the market at any price which will not only duplicate so quickly in quantity but that will also sort and fold. As a rule, two machines are required for this dual function and this creates not only a housing problem (I remember how little space you have for this operation) but necessitates two expenditures rather than one.

If you care to discuss this in further detail, let's chat about it when I stop by on Thursday or Friday of next week.

Cordially,

Incoming letter

A Tax Record Book

Just a word of thanks, gentlemen . . .

. . . for your inquiry about our income tax record book. A sample copy is being forwarded today in a separate envelope.

This record book, incidentally, was chosen by the Consolidated Electric Company for free distribution to all of its 9,000 office workers throughout the country. And dozens of other organizations have bought it in bulk because they want to help their employees keep accurate tax records and they feel our booklet does it in the most simple and specific form.

Attached is a price sheet which will give you volume discounts for orders in various quantities.

After you've received the record book, we'll welcome your comments.

Cordially,

Answering letter

Dear Mr. Van Vleet,

Thank you for sending along the income tax record book. It looks very interesting and useful to me. However, since I cannot make any decision on ordering these books for our employees, I have turned the book over to our accounting department for further study. If the men in that department feel as enthusiastic as I do about the book, I'm sure you'll be hearing from them.

Cordially,

Incoming letter

Dear Sirs,

I have just noticed your new advertisement of fishing tackle and other accessories in the latest *Sports Magazine*. Will you kindly send me the catalog mentioned in the ad? Thank you very much.

Sincerely,

Answering letter

After Request for Catalog

Dear Mr. Forman,

Several weeks ago, you wrote for our catalog and .we hoped by now to have received an order from you. There is no finer line of fishing tackle and accessories available. Every item, and the catalog lists some 500, is unconditionally guaranteed by us and you are promised satisfaction or your money back.

Is there some further information you'd like to have about any of the fine items listed in the catalog? I'll be happy to hear from you and answer any questions you care to ask. Or perhaps your order is already in the mail? If so, you're in for a lot of fishing pleasure—and chances are, THAT BIG ONE WON'T GET AWAY!

Cordially,

Incoming letter

A Free Sample

Dear Mr. Malloy,

The enclosed snapshot was taken in the lobby of the Hotel Vandermoor during the RAE convention two weeks ago. We were able to identify you because you wore the RAE badge. We hope you'll think it's a good likeness.

We used the new Pierpont X001 film for this snapshot, Mr. Malloy, and I think you'll admit there's a clarity that one doesn't often see in casual picture-taking.

If you'd like to try Pierpont X001 for yourself, just let us know by return mail. We'll be happy to send you a sample roll, without charge or obligation.

Cordially,

Answering letter

Dear Mr. Statler,

Thank you for the snapshot you took while I was attending the RAE convention. I think it is very good.

Please send me the sample of Pierpont X001. I'd like to try it out while I'm on my vacation next month.

Cordially,

Incoming letter

Inquiry About Lack of Orders

Dear Mr. Brown,

It's a long time since we had our last order from you. This worries me, since you have always been one of our most loyal customers and we have felt that a good and mutual satisfaction existed between us.

Was there anything wrong with our last shipment? If so, won't you please let us know so we can rectify the situation?

Is someone else taking care of your needs? If so, we'd like to know where we failed. Won't you please tell us?

If, on the other hand, it's simply a matter of business being a little slow, let me know that, too, won't you? We can offer you delayed payment on your next shipment, if you wish, and that way you can keep your stock completely up-to-date.

I'd appreciate hearing from you sometime soon.

Cordially,

Answering letter

Dear Mr. Edmund,

To put your mind at ease—I have only just returned to the U.S.A. after a wonderful five-month trip around the world. Please do not worry that Edmund's has failed me in any way. I shall be in to see you soon.

Cordially,

Incoming letter

A Gimmick Sales Letter

Dear Movie-Goer,

The tiny pledget of mink attached to this paper is simply your neighborhood movie theatre's way of reminding you that the forthcoming picture, *That Touch of Mink*, starring Doris Day and Cary Grant, is getting critics' raves wherever it is shown.

That Touch of Mink is a love story, a laugh story, a lilting story. It's done in gorgeous colorama and Miss Day's clothes are especially designed by the famous Ardine of Hollywood.

You mustn't miss this picture which starts at your neighborhood movie house on Wednesday, April 2nd and runs through Sunday, April 6th. There are two shows a day—a matinee at 2:30 every afternoon, and the evening performance at 8:30.

Be sure to see Mr. Grant and Miss Day—in one of their finest!

Answering letter

Dear Mr. Schneider,

Congratulations on a very clever idea—a "mink" reminder. I'm sure the picture *That Touch of Mink* is deserving of this promotion in addition to the fact that the picture seems to be the critics' choice.

You can count on my being there for the first matinee!

Cordially,

Incoming letter

Before a Visit in Person

Dear Stan,

It was good talking with you again and I'm delighted to learn how happy you are out in Mineola. From time to time, I do call on a few other firms in the area and I'll make it a point to stop in to see you on my next trip, which will probably be early next month.

I'm glad you're studying the book market and I'd like you to consider the effectiveness of our publication where it relates to the sale of the more "cultural" type of book.

First, look at the enclosed readership study, will you? In particular I refer you to page 5, showing the vital statistics of our readers, and, perhaps more importantly for your purpose, page 18 where it shows that reading is the most active hobby engaged in by these subscribers. Notice that more than 50% purchase and read better than ten books a year, a figure which is, as you know, unusually high.

This unique cultural audience is yours for less than $13 per thousand, Stan. You can buy advertising space elsewhere for much less per thousand, I'm sure you know. But you can't buy this kind of a dedicated reader for so little *anywhere*.

If you have any questions before my visit, just drop me a line. Otherwise, I'll see you around the 5th of March.

Cordially,

Answering letter

Dear Harry,

I'll be glad to see you on your next visit to Long Island. If you can give me a call a little in advance, perhaps we can have lunch together.

The readership study you sent is full of important information. However, I wonder what age group it covers. Are teenagers included—or did you cover only adult readers?

Cordially,

Incoming letter

Selling with a Gimmick

Dear Mr. Delatour,

This small bag of salt is just by way of a reminder that it's been a long time since we've had the pleasure of your company here at the Hotel Nash in Salt Lake City.

Our records show that you haven't been our guest since early in 1963. We hope you're headed our way soon, because we know you'll like what we've done to modernize our guest rooms, our lobby and our restaurants.

You'll be happy to know, too, that, in spite of a complete renovation of guest accommodations, there has been *no* renovation of rates.

I hope the little bag of salt will serve to remind you that there is comfort and even luxury, at economy prices, waiting for you in Salt Lake City.

Cordially,

Answering letter

Dear Mr. Sanders,

Thank you very much for the bag of salt. My travels haven't brought me to Salt Lake City for some time, but I do expect to be there in about six months. You can expect to hear from me shortly before that time.

Cordially,

Incoming letter

Asking for Time for Personal Visit

Dear Mr. Dante,

We've done some extemporaneous studies in 500 homes in 12 key cities and I think the enclosed reports will prove of interest to you.

You'll note on page 3 of the report that only 3% of these homes have had the services of a decorator and only

1.4% have had custom-made draperies or curtains installed. Keep in mind that the homes surveyed are owned by higher income citizens, all in the above-$10,000-a-year category.

Just visualize the huge untapped market that exists for decorators like you! Only the surface has been skimmed so far, in spite of the fact that, for instance, custom-made drapes can cost less than the ready-made variety, depending on fabric selected.

If you'd like us to do a study of this sort in a particular residential area of the city, we'll be happy to discuss costs with you. This is a bonafide method of lining up new customers and I think you'll be surprised at how much helpful information we can develop for you for a very small expenditure.

Will you let us know when it will be convenient for our representative, John Charles Wells, to stop in for a chat?

Cordially,

Answering letter

Dear Mr. Shapiro,

The information in your letter of July 3rd is just what I've been looking for so that we can try to develop a stronger sales approach. I would very much like to see your representative soon, for I have more questions to ask him.

Will you have Mr. Wells call me for an appointment early next week, please?

Cordially,

Incoming letter

A Sample of Product

Dear Miss Roberts,

The enclosed clipping, plasticized, comes to you with our compliments and sincere good wishes upon the announcement of your engagement.

The plasticized clipping will give you a small idea, happy bride-to-be, of just how beautifully plasticoating can preserve and protect the photographs taken of your wedding ceremony and reception.

Plasticizing is not at all expensive and we'll be happy to send our representative to see you about taking your wedding pictures and encasing them beautifully—for a lifetime—in plastic.

Please let us know by return mail when it will be convenient for our representative to visit you at your home. Evening visits are possible, if you so desire.

Very truly yours,

Answering letter

Dear Mr. Aigner,

I'm very much interested in having some photographs plasticized. Please have your representative call at my home on Tuesday evening, July the 9th.

Sincerely,

Incoming letter

Offering Information—Pamphlet

Dear Mr. Smith,

Do you realize that every state in the Union has different regulations in connection with the sale of liquor? And do you know that there are continual movements under foot to reinstate the prohibition laws which failed so miserably about a quarter of a century ago?

We have just published a pamphlet outlining the rules which apply in each of the 50 states to do with obtaining a license to sell liquor. It is the belief of our committee that a federal liquor law, which unifies the sale of liquor regulations in all states, would help to eliminate some of the complaints about alcohol which set off many of the urgent campaigns to stop the sale of liquor in the United States.

As a member of the Alcohol and Liquor Board of the State of Pennsylvania, you will find this pamphlet to be of interest. If you'd like a copy, just send a quarter in the enclosed envelope today. After you've read the pamphlet, we would appreciate your comments.

Cordially,

Answering letter

Dear Sirs,

Yes, I am anxious to read all about the laws governing the sale of liquor in the United States. Enclosed is my check for $1, for which please send me four copies of your pamphlet. I'm going to pass them on to some of my friends who are also interested.

Cordially,

Incoming letter

Selling by Mail

Dear Mrs. Little,

Just look at the attached picture, Mrs. Little! It shows you, in miniature, what a Travis Key Board is like. And it won't take very much imagination on your part, I'm sure, to realize how useful this could be in your work at the Post Office.

The Travis Key Board not only gives you an easy-to-identify spot to hang every key that you use in your work, but it has the unique feature of a combination lock which enables the owner to secure it for the night. Like a miniature safe, the Key Board cannot be opened unless you know the combination.

Enclosed are a few statements from other postmasters who find the Travis Key Board a great convenience. You can own one for only $17.50. Why not fill in the attached order blank today? We'll bill you later, if you wish.

Cordially,

Answering letter

Dear Sirs,

Thank you for sending the information on the Travis Key Board. It looks as if it is just what is needed here in the Martinville Post Office.

I have passed the order blank along to Mrs. Thomas Welch, who has just taken over the duties of Postmistress. Please remove my name from your mailing list.

Cordially,

Incoming letter

A Catalog

DO YOU HATE TO PUSH YOUR WAY THROUGH CROWDS?
DO YOU DISLIKE WAITING TO BE SERVED?
DO YOU FIND THAT SHOPPING TIME IS AT A PREMIUM?

If your answer is "yes" to any or all of those three questions, Gaylord Catalog shopping is for you.

The Gaylord Company for 52 years has been mailing its catalog, "A Department Store in Print," without charge to interested shoppers. This year's Catalog, with 527 colorful and descriptive pages, offers enthusiastic Gaylord shoppers a total of 6,001 items of clothing for the family. Sizes and prices are indicated for every item and many items are pictured in actual color to take the guesswork out of your purchasing decisions.

The Gaylord policy of "quality merchandise with prompt service for less" means that you can do your family and gift clothing shopping without leaving your home, without being shoved around, without waiting in line for a clerk. It also means that you can enjoy a tidy saving on everything you buy.

The Gaylord catalog is yours by return mail if you'll just fill in the attached postage-paid postcard with your name and address. Credit terms are available, too. If you want to take advantage of them, just check the box marked "Budget Payments."

We'd like to take you into the Gaylord family, so do mail the postcard back to us without delay. Our catalog will be mailed to you promptly and without obligation.

Answering letter

Dear Sirs,

In this remote area of northern Wyoming, I'm very much in need of such a catalog as yours since I am too far from a city of any size where I can have any worthwhile selection of merchandise to choose from. I have filled in the enclosed card and hope you can get your catalog off to me without delay.

Since I have friends who may also be interested in your catalog—will you kindly send me four more cards which I will pass along to them?

Thank you very much.

Cordially,

Incoming letter

To a Dealer

Dear Mr. Wright,

I have recently been named distributor for the Endicott Paint Company and can save you a good deal of money on outside white house paint, of which you sell such a considerable amount.

Endicott is out with a new product with a latex base which they call *Colonial White!* It has already been used extensively by contractors in New England, who like its slightly off-white qualities when they are repainting older homes. The off-white characteristic was built in because so many people objected to the stark-white new look of most white paints on the market today. This dazzling white, in the opinion of many, does not lend itself well to the older, colonial type home.

Colonial White is only available in gallons, but because of this we are able to offer it to you in dozen gallon lots at only $62.50 net. List price recommended is $7.80 per gallon. There are few reliable outside paints on the market today for under $8.95 a gallon.

I know you'll be able to turn over a quantity of *Colonial White*, so I have taken the liberty of shipping you a dozen gallons today. As an introductory offer, we'll absorb the $2.11 shipping charge on this first order. I know you'll be re-ordering soon.

                                        Cordially,

Answering letter

Dear Mr. Hall,

The dozen gallons of *Colonial White* arrived and within 24 hours one of our local contractors took the whole lot.

Will you please ship two dozen more gallons right away? I'm sure I won't have any problem selling it during the painting season.

Cordially,

Incoming letter

**Improvement in Merchandise and
Packaging Methods**

Dear Mr. Fennerman,

Some months ago, you complained about the difficulty you had in keeping nail polish remover from evaporating. That's why, you will recall, you were buying it in small containers and so were paying more than if you had bought in half gallon sizes.

Now, I'm happy to tell you, we have improved our nail polish remover by adding a special ingredient which prevents evaporation. The price is only seven cents a gallon more than our previous mixture. This will make it possible for you to buy the larger size from now on, without the loss which you previously suffered every time you opened the jug to refill your smaller containers.

I'm sure you'll want to order some of this improved remover right away. If you'll fill in the enclosed card and mail it back to me, I'll be able to make delivery next week when I make my usual call at your office.

Cordially,

Answering letter

Dear Sirs,

I've wanted to write you for some time now to tell you how pleased I am with your new nail polish remover. The added cost of seven cents a gallon seems like very little to pay when we can eliminate evaporation loss.

I'll be in touch with you just as soon as our present supply gets a little low.

Cordially,

Incoming letter

Easy Payment Plan

THIS IS IMPORTANT TO *YOU*, Mr. Store Manager!

With only 32 more shopping days until Christmas, your inventory is probably running low on many items and yet you're a little hesitant to buy more merchandise at this time with the need to charge it into 1964.

Well, no need to do it like that! Hudson Finance's new delayed payment plan makes it possible for you to order and stock up now and pay well after 1965 is under way. All you have to do is sign up for this plan with us and send us your invoices as they reach you for the merchandise you put in for Christmas. We'll pay them promptly, giving you the advantage of the usual 2% cash discount. You pay us after 90 days, and our charge to you is a minimal 1%.

How can we do it? Well, frankly, it's in the nature of an introduction to you. After this initial experiment, we're sure you'll want to take advantage of Hudson's regular floor plan financing. The enclosed brochure will tell you all about it.

One of our representatives will be in your neighborhood next Monday. He'll stop in to say hello and to familiarize you in complete detail with the entire Hudson Finance operation. But don't wait! Meantime, send in your authorization to start the special Christmas plan at once. That way you'll be adequately stocked up for holiday buying, and we'll pay the bills!

Cordially,

Answering letter

Dear Sirs,

I'm very interested in Hudson Finance's new delayed payment plan and I want to discuss this further with your representative. However, since I will not be in my shop on Monday, will you please send him over on Tuesday or Wednesday? I'll be in all day except for a brief period at lunch time.

Cordially,

Incoming letter

Better Insurance Coverage

Dear Customer,

The attached clipping will give you an indication of the kind of verdicts juries are influencing these days in cases of automobile accidents where physical injuries and disabilities are suffered. The $100,000 damage suit is being won more and more often in the state of New York.

That's why I think you'll want to give very thoughtful consideration to your present accident policy with us. It limits, as you know, the insurance company's liability to $50,000 which could mean under certain circumstances that you, personally, would be liable for an additional sum should you be unfortunately involved in an accident damage suit.

It does not cost very much to add an additional $50,000 coverage to the policy which is now in force. Certainly the added protection and security is well worth the extra $37 a year.

I hope you'll agree that the small additional premium will be very well budgeted when you consider the advantages it offers. If you do, you need only sign your name to the bottom of this letter and mail it back to me. Your additional coverage will be put into force at once.

Cordially,

Answering letter

Dear Sirs,

I'm returning your letter about the additional $50,000 coverage to my present accident policy—with my signature at the bottom of the letter.

Since I will be away for the next four months and will not be driving my automobile, I won't be in the market for this additional insurance until after my return to Scarsdale.

Will you have your representative call me in September for an appointment, please?

Cordially,

Incoming letter

Advantageous Sale of Merchandise

Dear Mr. Brown,

With prices on just about everything going up, *up, up!* . . . it gives me extreme pleasure to tell you that the trend is in the opposite direction here at the Manning Company.

We started a special campaign a year ago this month, an extreme effort on the part of every department head to cut the cost of overhead. This campaign has been so successful that we are now able to reflect its results in concrete savings to our customers.

Now you can purchase a Manning No. 707 tenderizer

machine for only $392, a full $50 less than it would have cost a month ago. This saving means that you can start at once to place these machines in every one of your kitchens and that you can complete your plan to tenderize "every piece of beef served" by your restaurants much sooner than you had planned.

As a matter of fact, the sales manager has just okayed my suggestion that we offer you an additional $25 discount on each machine if you purchase more than 10 at one time.

Please give this your very prompt consideration. Machines for immediate delivery are at a premium, but I do have 40 of them reserved for you and will hold them for another week, until you have time to get back to me with your order.

Cordially,

Answering letter

Dear Mr. Greenberg,

Please do not hold the 40 Manning No. 707 tenderizer machines for me because I do not plan to make any further investment in equipment at this time.

I'll be in touch with you if I am able to make a decision about this in the future.

Cordially,

Incoming letter

Advertising—Coupons

Dear Mr. Bronson,

When we detailed to you in our letter of February 11th the new achievement plan, we hoped for an expression of approval from you. Is it possible that our letter never reached **you?**

Just in case that is so, let me outline again the thinking behind the new plan, which has been nicknamed AP—standing, of course, for Achievement Plan.

In summary, it's a plan to help you sell new eyeglasses to people who are already wearing glasses. Actually, it's nothing more than a plan to follow-up on your customers as well as to encourage newcomers to visit your office.

The enclosed series of ads will be financed by us, when you run them in your local paper. Each ad, you will note, is coded so that you can tell what results are obtained. The theme of the entire series is "Eyeglasses can add to your appearance and attractiveness."

Each time you run an ad, just send us the tearsheet from your local newspaper, accompanied by a list of names of those who returned the coded coupons to you. We'll follow up for you with a mailing similar to the enclosed. Then, as customers who've received our literature come into your store and make their purchases, ask them to fill in their names and addresses on the warranty cards you always use. Send in those warranty cards as usual. Where the name on any one matches the name of someone who already answered your ad via the coupon, we'll credit you with $10.

A store manager in Denver has already piled up a credit of $300 in this fashion. Another in Wilmington, Delaware is on his way to the $500 mark. You can benefit, too.

So why not get in on the plan today? All you need do is drop me a line telling me you want to participate and then notify me when the first ad will run. I certainly hope to hear from you in short order.

Cordially,

Answering letter

Dear Mr. Granville,

I'm very interested in your Achievement Plan for selling eyeglasses, and want to participate. I will run the first advertisement in the local newspaper on Monday, July 6th, and will get a tearsheet off to you at that time, along with a list of names of people who return the coupons to me.

Thank you for writing about this. It sounds like a great plan.

Cordially,

XIV

Letters OF GOOD WILL

❦ Good will is nothing more than an attitude—an attitude of kindliness toward a person or an organization. And while a company's success or failure is largely dependent upon the products or services it offers, in a world full of competitive products, it's helpful when a client or customer looks upon you and your company with a favoring eye. Good will is actually built from good public relations and such relations can be achieved frequently by attentions sometimes neglected in the frantic business climate. The letters included here are written solely from the point of establishing fine public relations.

CHECK LIST

FOR LETTERS OF GOOD WILL

1. Express approval for something your correspondent has accomplished, if possible.

2. Offer assistance without any hope of immediate reward.
3. Do *more* than is expected of you.

Incoming letter

Dear Mr. Littleford,

Last year you sent a letter to customers and others who deal with your company outlining your policy in connection with Christmas gifts to your employees.

Will you please send me a copy of that letter?

Cordially,

Answering letter

Christmas Gift Policy

THE BILLBOARD PUBLISHING COMPANY

165 WEST 46th STREET

NEW YORK, N. Y., 10036

W. D. LITTLEFORD
PRESIDENT

To All Our Friends:

With the Christmas season approaching
it is once again time for us to remind our friends
to refrain from sending Christmas gifts to any
employees of The Billboard Publishing Company.

This message is being sent to suppliers of
our recently acquired magazines, Modern Photography
and Carnegie Hall Program for the first time, and
again includes the business friends of Vend, High
Fidelity, Billboard, Amusement Business, American
Artist, and Watson-Guptill Publications, Inc.

Employees as well as management agree on this
policy, and you can therefore, avoid embarrassment and
the need for returning gifts if you rely solely on the
Christmas card to keep the holiday spirit alive.

The least we ask is that our staff members
receive only those gifts that are of such modest
value that they are distributed generally by you to
numerous friends and customers.

We firmly believe that it is necessary to
eliminate all practices which can be the cause of any
suspicion whatsoever of a conflict of interest. Therefore, please help us.

May I personally take this occasion to wish you
the greetings of the season on behalf of all the staff
members of The Billboard Publishing Company.

Sincerely,

W. D. Littleford

WDL:av

Incoming letter

Lost Articles

Dear Mr. Moore,

I took Flight 104 out of Boston last Tuesday and arrived in New York safely, but without my trusty old briefcase. The only identification I can offer you is the fact that it was oxford leather and bore my initials R.W. inside of it (and it was not locked). Inside were several letters addressed to me as well as a clean white shirt and an electric shaver.

Since the briefcase and I are old friends, I'd like to see it again. Will you see if your Lost and Found Department can track it down for me?

Cordially,

Answering letter

Dear Mr. Wilson,

You're about to renew a pleasant and long-standing acquaintance! Your briefcase is on its way to you via American Express and should be delivered shortly. It was found between two seats on the plane and seems not to have suffered from its brief and extemporaneous solo.

Thanks for using Airjet—briefcase and all.

Cordially,

Incoming letter

Offer of Free News Service

Dear Miss Blankenhorn,

Here's a copy of our latest newsletter. And while newsletters are seemingly a dime a dozen, I think this one will keep you more up-to-date on our industry than anything else you've seen.

If you'd like to receive the newsletter every month, just drop me a note and I'll put your name on our regular mailing list. No charge, of course!

Cordially,

Answering letter

Dear Sirs,

I find that after going over your latest newsletter carefully, it is exactly what I need during these busy times.

Please put me on your regular mailing list.

Cordially,

Incoming letter

Gratitude for Advice

Dear Mr. Mencken,

It is just five years ago that I sat with you in your office and consulted with you about my future. I'm sure you'll recall how uncertain I was but I'm not sure if you realize how very helpful you were.

I took your advice and have been so grateful that I did. As you can see from the stationery on which this is written, I made a connection with this organization right after our chat. It was the best thing I've ever done. The work is interesting, my associates are friendly and gracious, and I honestly believe my future lies right here.

Right now, with the holidays so near, I thought it might not be amiss to drop you this note expressing my gratitude.

I hope that you and your family will have a happy Christmas Season and a prosperous, healthful New Yea.:.

Sincerely,

Answering letter

Dear Albert,

It was kind and thoughtful of you to write me and let me know about your good fortune at Scandia, Inc. Of course, it does not surprise me, because I well remembeı your record here at the University, as well as your popularity among the students.

My family and I plan to spend the holidays right here on the campus. If you should be up this way visiting your parents, please drop in to see us.

Kindest regards and best wishes for the holiaay season.

Cordially,

Incoming letter

To Secretary on Vacation

Dear Mary,

I'm so used to having you do all my correspondence that I must admit it's a struggle to sit down at the typewriter and peck out a note on my own. But I just wanted you to know that your fine and devoted work during the past year has been much appreciated.

I hope that you and Trend are enjoying a very happy holiday season and vacation in the South. You both deserve a good rest and I trust the weatherman will cooperate to make your stay at Daytona the very greatest.

Sincerely,

Answering letter

Dear Mrs. Archer,

Your thoughtful letter arrived here just after we did last night. I just want to say thank you very much. I will write more after we settle down a bit and I'll have time to concentrate on a letter. In the meantime, please call me if there is anything you need me for. Just leave a message if I'm not in. We expect to spend a great deal of time at the beach.

Happy holidays to you and your family,

Sincerely,

Incoming letter

Need for Publication

45 EAST 51st STREET
NEW YORK 22, N.Y
PLAZA 5-1420

·

WASHINGTON 6, D C

·

GREENWICH, CONN

FAIRBANKS ASSOCIATES INC.
MANAGEMENT CONSULTANTS

March 19, 1963

Mrs. Claire N. Eddings
Director of Advertising Sales
High Fidelity
Great Barrington, Massachusetts

Dear Mrs. Eddings:

A good secretary can be a priceless asset to the company
executive. The secretary's value to the executive will
depend largely on how he has trained her. A secretary
who is a barrier instead of a bridge, in many cases,
insulates the executive from contacts with other people
in an undesirable manner.

It is important that a secretary know explicitly how her
boss wishes her to handle his business. It is important
that the executive be consistent and that he set an example
for her to follow. Having a secretary that works with an
executive is far more effective than one who works <u>for</u> an
executive.

These statements may explain why we sometimes find execu-
tives with full-time, qualified secretaries and who do not
receive maximum relief to net more from their executive
efforts.

Very truly yours,

John J. Evans

John J. Evans
President

JJE:MH

MEMBERS OF THE ASSOCIATION OF CONSULTING MANAGEMENT ENGINEERS

Answering letter

Dear Mr. Evans,

Thanks so much for your very encouraging letter. The secretary's importance in the world of business is no longer an intangible thing. Day after day and year after year, men like you are leaning more and more on the secretary for assistance in their work. Yet far too often, the secretary is expected to handle matters for which he or she has not been thoroughly trained. That's why both Prentice-Hall and I believe that the forthcoming book will prove extremely useful as a guide to the writing of better and better letters. We're so glad you agree with us.

Cordially,

Incoming letter

Request for Future Needs

Dear Miss Goodman,

Thank you for helping us make the year 1964 the most successful in our history. As you know, our sales surpassed those of any previous year and the increased business made it possible for us to move into our new headquarters sooner than we had anticipated. This, in turn, will enable us to offer you better and more efficient service than ever before. We couldn't have done it without your valued business.

So that we may fill your orders promptly during 1965, will you be able to give us an estimate of your needs for the next 12 months?

Please accept our heartiest wishes for a Happy New Year!

Sincerely,

Answering letter

Dear Mr. Schwab,

All of us here at Spring Gadgets, Inc. are happy to learn of your increased business in 1964. It has been a pleasure to deal with you this past year and we are looking forward to an even better year in 1965!

An analysis of our sales here shows a 15 percent increase, and that indicates that we will be increasing our orders by at least that amount in 1965.

Kindest regards and all good wishes for the coming year.

Cordially,

Incoming letter

Assistance on Insurance Coverage

Dear Claire,

Glad to send along your copy of the Homeowners policy on your new residence for the same benefits as before but with reduced amounts as shown on the bill. Please review these figures and do let me know if any should be changed.

Also enclosed is your policy for moving the furnishing; it was written with a November 27th date, but this is amended by an endorsement inside the policy to November 26th.

The Homeowners policy, HOU 105656, on the Maple Avenue house, should be returned promptly for the return premium credit. There will be a considerable refund and you might wish to defer payment of the two policies until the company advises me of this credit.

Thank you, Claire, for continuing this insurance privilege with us. We will welcome any questions you may have.

Cordially,

Answering letter

Dear Joe,

Looking at the figures on the Homeowners policy, I believe all is in order. I can't think of a thing that should be changed at this time.

With this letter I'm returning the old policy for credit. I will take advantage of your kind offer to defer payment of the two new policies until you find out how much credit is due me.

Thank you so much for doing a good job for me again I'll be away all next week, so if there is anything else to be tended to, call me right after that.

Cordially,

Incoming letter

To an Employee

Dear Sam,

It's been a tough year, but an exciting one—and the fact that we go into 1965 in such good shape is due to a very large extent to your unstinting efforts.

I realize that a simple "thank you" isn't very much, but I hope you'll understand that it comes from the bottom of my heart. We're lucky and proud that you're on our team, and I hope that next year the thanks can be in the form of something more concrete (such as money).

Meantime, I hope you and yours will enjoy every minute of the new year and that you and Diana will be able to drop in for a drink on New Year's Eve.

Cordially,

Answering letter

Dear Chuck,

Thank you for your letter which I received in this morning's mail. It's wonderful of you to give me so much credit for our successful year, and I want to say at this time that I've never been so happy on any other job. I have you to thank for that.

Diana and I would love to stop in for a drink with you on New Year's Eve, but we won't return from Columbus until early on the morning of the 2nd. May we have a rain check please?

Happy New Year to you and yours.

Sincerely,

Incoming letter

To a Customer

Dear Mr. Taylor,

As the holiday season opens, I can't help but think how much of my enjoyment of it is due to the fine relationship we at Owens Mills have with our good customers like you.

Business is supposed to be a cold-blooded proposition, but our dealings with you have always been warm and understanding. Because we're human, we've made a few goofs along the way, but you were always willing to listen to our reasons and give us an opportunity to make corrections where we could.

We've been doing business with you at Taylor for almost seven years, believe it or not. And always we have come away with the feeling that you are one of the nicest guys in the trade.

Perhaps knowing how we feel will help to add to your enjoyment of the forthcoming holidays. I hope so. And, of course, we wish the best in the year ahead for you and your family.

Sincerely,

Answering letter

Dear Mr. Hamilton,

Thank you very much for your kind letter of the 14th. It reached me on this remote island of Cinnebar the day after Christmas, where I'm enjoying a few days at the edge of the jungle.

As soon as I return from my holiday, I'll be in touch with you so that we can have lunch together, and talk over some of our 1965 business prospects.

May the New Year bring you peace, prosperity and happiness.

Cordially,

Incoming letter

Dear Mr. Woodstock,

On Monday last, I received your bill for the 10 shares of General Supply which you bought for me. I sent my check by return mail. As of today—10 days later—I have not received my certificate.

Will you look into this and let me know when to expect it, please?

Cordially,

Answering letter

To a Customer

Dear Mr. Teller,

The transfer of 10 shares of General Supply stock is at the transferee's office at the present time and should be mailed to your address in your name very shortly.

I'd like to take this occasion to thank you for this business and to wish you a very Merry Christmas and Happy New Year. I trust that we shall have the pleasure of seeing these 10 shares of stock grow to many more in the years ahead.

Very truly yours,

Incoming letter

Welcome to New Employee

Dear Dr. Jansen,

For a long time, I've been one of your admirers and extremely interested in the work you've done in cancer research.

Now, I'm so pleased to learn that you are joining our research laboratory as consultant. You'll be working with many of the nice people I've known for years and I'm confident you'll find them all intelligent, able co-workers.

After you get set in your office, let's try to grab an hour for lunch. In the meantime, if I can be helpful in any way, just pick up your interoffice phone and let me know.

Sincerely,

Answering letter

Dear Dr. Brooks,

Thank you for your letter of welcome. I am really very pleased to be a part of your fine research organization.

How about lunch at 1:00 o'clock on Monday in the cafeteria? There are some questions I'd like to ask you and it will be fine to have a chat.

Cordially,

Incoming letter

Dear Carol,

You told me last week that your "Birthday Letter" was just about ready. I hope we will have it by Monday so we can place it in the best spot in Thursday's *Courier*. Will you let me know right away, please?

Cordially,

Answering letter

A Business Birthday Letter

Dear Friends,

It doesn't seem possible a full year has passed since I stood on Main Street, watching the bright, new red and white sign being lifted into place, announcing to one and all—the opening of Carousel.

Carousel was a big venture for our family. My husband's job as teacher and coach, our son's daily activities, my job with Sally Dean, had always been enough to busy our lives. On last March first, we had an additional and big responsibility—to take care of the new member of the family and be sure Carousel brought joy to those who were kind enough to come through its door.

The year holds many memories. Most memorable are the children themselves; watching them color and read at the table and chairs and sharing the enthusiasm of "the artist of the week," coming in to draw his or her wish on our blackboard, proudly signing it with name and age, and leaving it for all to see during a week. The board is now booked so far in advance we send reminder cards.

I don't know what we would do without "Trigger Horse," originally named and owned by our son. When he outgrew the horse, we all regretted putting it in the attic pasture. This last year has brought "Trigger" out of retirement. Once again he takes children for many rides each day.

Two animals the children play with are "Sumantha Turtle" and "Dear Duck," whom we could never part with because he sings one note—off-key. They have become considerably banged up of course, and one little girl, concerned with a "boo-boo" on Sumantha's head, left reluctantly but returned the next day and tenderly placed a *Bandaid* over the turtle's hurt spot. She left smiling. All this done without a word spoken.

What happy expressions on the faces of those who made visits at Thanksgiving to stand and stare in amazement at the life-sized Steif lion and tiger. The animals have promised to take a two-week vacation from their East Hartford home and spend it with us each November. They like the lollipop tree. It waits for them and all the children to choose a lollipop from its branches.

We can't forget the little girl who went from one dress to another, asking, "What size is this, mommy? What size is this one?" Mother didn't answer the questions. Finally the four-year-old said frantically, "Is this one Size ME?"

Trying on dresses, a young lady found one that also met the approval of mother. She calmly walked over to her younger sister: "Would you like to grow into this one?"

Boys are very casual about buying clothes. Bored, I guess, is a better word. Parents seem to feel it is more fun to dress a girl than a boy, and it is harder to find nice boys' clothing. Having always bought for a son, I personally enjoy shopping for boys' clothes, particularly when I find some that can take the beating we all know they will get and still look good. Anyhow, boys don't seem to mind if Mom just looks. They are very good at discovering the lollipop tree, have drawn some of the most outstanding pictures on the blackboard, and take the longest trips on Trigger by far.

Although we can't invite you all to one big party, a birthday table is set in our window. In attendance are Teddy Bear, Sumantha Turtle, Dachshund Dog, Rein-Deer, Musical Donkey, and of course at the head of the table, our two marvelous white dogs, who have become a part of almost every window. They model hats frequently and find the necessity of sun glasses when the glare from the street becomes too bright. They play with blocks, marbles, scrabble, have sock fights, and even try to win prizes. In last summer's kennel club show, they didn't win anything; but curlers, nail clippers, dog brushes, hair nets, and mirrors cluttered the window. They enjoyed the Memorial Day parade with a group of animal friends (since placed in fine homes), and the Fourth of July picnic again filled the window, this time with all kinds of food. Sir Walrus sipping chocolate milk from a bottle through a straw is a sight we won't forget for awhile. At Christmas time the two white dogs hung their stocking in the window. They have certainly earned a permanent home here.

Have you noticed the painting on our wall of the clown and duck? How we got it is a story of unusual generosity. One day one of my favorite summer customers admired the stuffed clown and duck. She asked if she might borrow them both to paint. Not even knowing she could draw, I said yes. Two days later she returned with a handsome oil painting and there on canvas was the duck, just having knocked over a pot of flowers and making the clown laugh. She captured their personalities perfectly and *gave* the store a valued treasure.

With one year gone we start the seasons all over again. Some of the bathing suits are here (can't wait for the baby bikini with the daisy on the seat of the pants)! Boys' cruise clothes have been purchased for trips to Bermuda, Florida, and the Virgin Islands. Easter is right around the corner and the hats will soon be arriving, along with dresses, suits and gloves. Spring is definitely peeking through!

For the fun and first year success of Carousel, we are

grateful to all of you who came from near and far to shop with us. You have made my job of serving you a real pleasure. The red carpet on our front door step has also weathered the year nicely. It is there to say welcome, and we hope you will walk over it frequently in our second year.

Thank you.

Sincerely,

XV

Letters OF PERSUASION

ⓥ Nearly everyone in a key company position has developed his own ideas about what is best for his firm as it relates to his own area of responsibility and his staff. Sometimes these ideas are the result of trial and error. Sometimes they are based on innate conservatism, hostility toward a competitor or a forced managerial policy. Occasionally, these preconceived ideas constitute a barrier to progressive changes or to the natural elements of growth and development. They can cause businessmen to frown on suggestions made by others, even when these stem from a desire to improve business relations, upgrade company methods or make innovations of any sort.

Just as a psychologist uses a variety of techniques to break down the resistance of a patient or student, so must the letter-writer handle the case of the stubborn executive. If he thinks he is dealing with a matter of improper thinking, he must refrain from being blunt about saying so in his letters. Instead, he must use tactful and subtle methods to bring his correspondent around to recognizing for himself his short-sightedness. Included are examples of difficult situations, handled with careful forethought, designed not to offend or condemn, but rather to stimulate toward proper action.

CHECK LIST

FOR LETTERS OF PERSUASION

1. Get attention.
2. Create desire.
3. Get conviction.
4. Make request for action.

Incoming letter

Economy in Quantity Buying

Dear Customer,

There are more ways than one to lick the high cost of living. And for retailers like you, one of the most effective ways is to order in volume wherever possible in order to take advantage of quantity discounts.

Let me just analyze how this could have worked for you in 1964. Our records show that during the year just ended, you purchased 710 dozen assorted bulbs. Broken down, we show that this total was made up of 105 dozen 40-watt bulbs, 300 dozen 60-watt bulbs, and 305 dozen 100-watt bulbs. And since you never ordered more than 10 dozen of any of these at a single time, we had to process about 40 individual orders to serve you. In every case, you bought at the highest possible price, since discounts start to apply only at the 25-dozen level.

In batches of 25 dozen for each order, you could have cut your total purchase costs for the year by $625. Just imagine—$625 to take home with you as additional profits! And if you had ordered 50-dozen lots, you could have latched on to another $500 in profits.

If it's a question of terms, please remember that we're always ready and willing to cooperate with customers whose credit with us is satisfactory. Yours most certainly is. So why not let me send one of our salesmen in to see you next week to help you set up a system for 1965 which will help you earn the biggest possible discounts?

I hope to hear from you soon.

Cordially,

Answering letter

Dear Mr. Guidi,

It really hurts when I think of losing $625 last year. I wish this method of savings had been brought to my attention sooner. Now, I know the facts, and I'm passing them along to our Order Department. Just as soon as we have some figure on our 1965 estimated sales, we'll place an order to cover the needed light bulbs.

Cordially,

Incoming letter

Alleviating Fear

Dear Mr. Larkin,

This letter is being sent to you at your office for the obvious reason that we shouldn't let Mrs. Larkin see it.

In my opinion, and in the opinion of the two consultants whose reputations as diagnosticians are excellent, Mrs. Larkin requires surgery, and as quickly as possible.

It is understandable why you feel the way you do about surgery, Mr. Larkin. You expressed yourself very clearly about this when we first met. We feel that there isn't any other treatment, however, if you want your wife to recover her good health. Surgery isn't what it was 50 years ago—or even 10—and I'm sure you will be comforted in knowing that the mortality rate for this particular operation, when performed in time, is only five percent. The rate for neglect of this condition is an absolute 100 percent.

If it is at all possible for you and your wife to stop in at my office Monday evening at 8 o'clock, I would like to talk to you further. If it is not convenient, please call my secretary and arrange for another meeting within the next week.

Cordially,

Answering letter

Dear Dr. Schweitzer,

Thank you for your letter and further explanation of the surgery required by Mrs. Larkin. Now that I'm over the shock of being told of the seriousness of the disease, I can understand the importance of the necessary surgery.

I'll bring Mrs. Larkin to your office on Monday evening at 8 o'clock.

Cordially,

Incoming letter

Soliciting Advertising

Gentlemen,

You will be especially interested to know about the forthcoming February issue of *House Furnishings* Magazine.

The cover is designed to point up two exciting articles appearing in that issue on cabinetry and shelving in the home. Supporting illustrations and photographs will suggest numerous and varied ways for integrating these features into either new or existing decor.

The February issue will present a most unusual and timely opportunity to publicize your very fine products. As you know well from past experience, our 400,000 primary and secondary readers are your most likely prospective clients.

The closing date for the February issue is December 15th. Won't you let us hear from you right away, so that we can reserve a choice spot for you?

Cordially,

Answering letter

Dear Mr. Gilbert,

Your letter about the February issue of *House Furnishings* Magazine makes me think that issue would be ideal for the new ad we are preparing on our Medallion Custom Built Furniture.

Before we can make a final decision, will you please rush a copy of the December issue of *House Furnishings?* We want to study some of your editorial material again. Then we will let you know definitely about reserving space in the February issue.

Cordially,

Incoming letter

Subscription Renewal

"SORRY-I FORGOT!"

...one of our subscribers wrote us.

"I meant to renew -- but I just didn't get around to it. Thanks for the reminder."

You probably meant to renew, too...but didn't get around to it. Too busy with art, perhaps.

We have been sending you American Artist regularly so there's no great loss. But to make sure you miss no issues won't you please sign and return the enclosed card now?

And do keep in mind, the longer the term you specify, the more money you save!

Sincerely,

Walter F Grueninger

For American Artist

Grueninger/B

P.S. If you already renewed, please disregard this reminder.

American Artist   Subscription Dept. /2160 PATTERSON STREET/CINCINNATI 14, OHIO

Answering letter

Dear Mr. Grueninger,

Enclosed you will find my check for another three years' subscription to *American Artist*, along with the card showing my correct name and address.

Your artist's conception of the "Forgetful Artist" is an accurate description of what happened to me!

Cordially,

Incoming letter

To Clarify a Misunderstanding

Dear Gerry,

My letter to you regarding your present contract status was dictated on Friday, prior to a complete understanding with Terry and Robin that it would be to your advantage to complete your contract with February and March, rather than repeat an ad in January.

They both felt, and I agreed, that new products would be available which would make ads in those months more productive of sales.

Unfortunately, my original letter slipped through the dictating pool and I was not able to bring you up to date on our conversation. I'm writing this simply to dispel any confusion my earlier letter may have created.

Cordially,

Answering letter

Dear Mal,

Yes, I was confused after reading your first letter—but all is now clear, since I have received your letter of explanation, plus our telephone conversation.

The arrangement to complete our contract with February and March is quite satisfactory.

Cordially,

Incoming letter

Option on Real Estate

Dear Mr. Ardmore,

Two weeks ago, when we spent a day together examining the various parcels of land that were available in downtown Syracuse, I thought you were seriously interested in the tract on the corner of Tracy and Skidmore Avenues.

Now I find that, if we move quickly, it may be possible to close the deal for that parcel for about $4,000 less than the price I quoted. The reason for this is that the owners need to put themselves into a better cash position right away.

Naturally, at this new price, the property will appeal to many others and I believe it will move very, very rapidly. As a matter of fact, I have another interested party, but feel that you should have first refusal because your interest takes precedence.

However, I cannot remain inactive on this very long. The best I can do is to give you a five-day option, meaning that you must make up your mind by Friday, September 19th. I'd suggest, therefore, that you get in touch with me right away. I'm sure that this spot would be ideal for the purpose you have in mind. There aren't many attractive properties in good locations for this kind of money, as you know.

Will you let me hear from you right away, Mr. Ardmore?

Cordially,

Answering letter

Dear Mr. Lord,

I still am very interested in the tract at Tracy and Skid-more Avenues, and I will take you up on that five-day option. I'm still working on some figures which I need be-fore I can make a definite decision, but I'll phone you for sure on Thursday afternoon. Then we can talk about a meet-ing for Friday, when I expect to be in downtown Syracuse.

Cordially,

Incoming letter

Dear Mr. Minich,

I want to thank you very much for spending so much time with me on Wednesday. Your cordiality was much ap-preciated.

However, I have decided to float the loan elsewhere, because upon investigation I find that your interest rates are half of one percent higher than many of your competitors. Half of one percent over a period of five years on a sum of money the size of the loan I'm talking of can represent a pretty penny, indeed.

Thanks, nevertheless, for your kindness.

Cordially,

Answering letter

Additional Information

Dear Mr. Nelson,

I hope you have considered all the angles in connection with borrowing money for half of one percent less than the interest rate we offered you.

The saving of this half percent can often prove disastrous, Mr. Nelson. For example, there is no loan insurance connected with a loan at a lesser rate of interest. If you are unable to meet your obligations because of disability or through death, your property is immediately confiscated by the loan company unless you insure yourself elsewhere, and this is very costly, as you know.

Also, where loans are offered at a lesser rate of interest, you will find that the term of the loan is actually for only one year, and only renewable under certain circumstances for each additional year of the five. What would happen if at the end of one year—or two—you could not renew the loan and were unable to pay up the remaining balance? Not a very pretty kettle of fish, is it?

I hope you'll study this matter much more carefully before you make your final decision. Mandalay also offers you an "open end" note, which means that you can pay it off in full at any time without penalty. There are many advantages here, too, as I'm sure you will agree.

I'll phone you in a day or two to chat some more. I'm convinced that it is in your best interests for the long-term picture for you to borrow the Mandalay way.

Cordially,

Incoming letter

Statistical Information

Good Morning, Mr. Smith,

If you don't have safety belts on your car, you'll be interested in the attached news story clipped from last Sunday's *Times*. The story, you will note, is the result of a study made for a full 12-month period by Bureaus of Motor Vehicle Registry in seven of our more heavily populated cities.

The study showed that 60 percent less physical injury was suffered by drivers and passengers in cars that were equipped with safety belts where the safety belts were in use at the time of an accident.

The mortality rate for safety belt users involved in motor accidents was 39 percent less than where no safety belts were in use.

As the result of these studies, 22 States will make the installation of safety belts compulsory in all cars manufactured after 1964.

We can equip your car with safety belts in jiffy time and for a very small sum. Just give us the go-ahead by return mail. Our serviceman will pick up your car, install safety belts, and return it to you in less than an hour. We will not bill you for 30 days.

Play it safer, Mr. Smith, with safety belts.

Yours very truly,

Answering letter

Dear Sirs,

I'll take you up on your offer. Will you please have your service man pick up my Falcon at my office, on Friday at 2:00 P.M., equip it with safety belts and return it to me in less than an hour?

Cordially,

XVI

Letters OF REQUEST

When writing a letter of request, it's helpful to remember that a certain element of persuasiveness, of salesmanship, must prevail to put the recipient into the proper mood to do what is asked. It's equally important to *be specific*. If you request an appointment, try to name alternate times and dates. If you request information, spell it out. Why do you want it? To what use will you put it? Do you expect to pay for it? Even if you request something so intangible as cooperation, try to explain just how this can be given, why you must have it, how it will benefit the man who receives your letter requesting it.

CHECK LIST
FOR LETTERS OF REQUEST

1. Tell why you need the material or help or information.

2. Tell exactly what you want.
3. Make it clear whether or not you expect to pay for it.
4. Give a time when you must have it.
5. Leave an opening for refusal of your request, if it is delicate.
6. Thank your correspondent in advance.

Incoming letter

Statistical Information

Dear Mr. Peebles,

The Marketing Director of this company, Mr. Stanley Hunt, has asked me to write you in the hope that you can supply some statistics in connection with the sale of sewing machines. He plans to incorporate the figures into a general market study he is making of motorized appliances for the home. Therefore, it would help if you can distinguish the total number of sewing machines sold for industrial purposes from those sold for use in the home. Mr. Hunt would, of course, give credit to your organization for the research responsible for the figures you give him in this connection. The study will be released under Mr. Hunt's by-line, in the November 6th issue of *Home Appliance* Magazine. In order to meet this deadline, your material must reach Mr. Hunt before September 1st.

Your help will be greatly appreciated. May we hear from you soon?

Cordially,

Answering letter

Dear Miss Smith,

I shall be glad to send Mr. Hunt the statistical material you asked for in your letter of the 19th. It is being prepared now and should reach him no later than August 15th. Tell him I'll look forward very much to seeing the story in *Home Appliance* Magazine. Please feel free to call me if Mr. Hunt has any questions after my material arrives.

Cordially,

Incoming letter

For Completion of Lists

Dear Mr. Winegard,

Would it be possible for you to send us the addresses of, and products sold by, the companies listed on the attached sheet?

We would appreciate anything you can do to get this information to us as soon as possible.

Cordially,

Answering letter

Dear Mr. Abel,

Answering your recent letter, I'm sorry to say that many of the companies listed on the sheet you sent me are unknown to me.

Is this a list of sugar and syrup manufacturers? If so, I suspect that it accidentally contains some names of distributors, too, and I know very few of these people.

I'm returning the list and have filled in the information

wherever I was able to. Drop me a line if there is anything more to discuss in this connection.

Cordially,

Incoming letter

For Listings

Dear Mr. Gurnsey,

On return to my desk after two weeks' vacation, I find among the accumulation of mail your letter of August 12th asking for the names and addresses of the firms which are members of the AOM.

In order not to unduly delay a reply, I'm enclosing the Directory Information data sheets which these firms sent in for listings in the 1962 AOM Dealer Show, which I think will supply the information you want in the quickest possible fashion.

If you can return these directory sheets to me when they have served your purpose, I would appreciate it.

Cordially,

Answering letter

Dear Mr. Roche,

Enclosed please find the Information Data sheets you sent to me last week.

Thank you very much for supplying me with this information in such a quick and helpful fashion. The sheets proved to be exactly what I needed and we took the liberty of making our own complete list of members from them.

Perhaps the enclosed extra copy of this list will prove useful to you.

Cordially,

Incoming letter

Additional Information Required

Dear Mr. Homer,

Thanks so much for the detailed schedule which you sent me on May 22nd in connection with the market survey we discussed. At this point, it sounds very interesting.

However, I'm disappointed that nowhere have you given me either dates or costs. As you know from our personal conversation, my decision will be based on the timeliness of this survey and I can only go ahead with it if it also fits into my very limited budget.

Before we go any further, will you get back to me with a calendar on the study—starting date and cut-off date —as well as a detailed price outline of costs for each phase as it completes itself? After that, I hope we can work toward a prompt decision.

Cordially,

Answering letter

Dear Mr. Schneider,

On the copy of the detailed schedule of the market survey, which is enclosed, I've filled in the information you require on dates as well as the cost outline on each phase as it is completed.

I hope the omission of this information has not inconvenienced you too much in making your decision. If there is any other way we can help, please let me know promptly.

Cordially,

Incoming letter

Extension of Option

Dear Mr. Muller,

As you know, this company has an option for space in the Better Living Pavilion at the World's Fair, and that option will expire next Monday, February 23rd.

Since it is impossible to hold a meeting of our directors until Tuesday, February 24th, and since this matter must be decided upon by these directors, will you be kind enough to extend our option to Thursday, February 26th? I hope to have a firm decision for you at that time.

Cordially,

Answering letter

Dear Mr. Hansen,

We will be very happy to extend your option on the space in the Better Living Pavilion until Thursday, February 26th. We will expect to hear from you at that time.

Cordially,

Incoming letter

Travel Literature

Dear Mr. Appleby,

An ad in last Sunday's *Times* indicated that a note to you would bring further information about the Hawaiian vacation you advertised. Will you be kind enough to forward

at once any available literature? I am very seriously considering a Hawaiian vacation in early May.

Cordially,

Answering letter

Dear Mrs. Angel,

Thank you very much indeed for your inquiry and for
your interest in Martin's Hawaiian vacation as advertised in
the Sunday *Times*.

It is our pleasure to enclose the literature you requested.
We hope it will give you the first taste of an exciting holiday
as well as induce you to experience personally the magical
adventure of a vacation in the Islands.

If you have any questions or desire further information,
please do not hesitate to contact us here at Martin's.

Sincerely yours,

Incoming letter

Cost of Trip

Dear Mr. Tollin,

Your ad in last Sunday's *Times* neglected to mention the
price of the Hawaiian vacation you advertised. I'd appreciate
an immediate reply from you telling the costs of such a trip,
economy class and first class. My wife and I are thinking
seriously of a vacation in Hawaii this spring and will be
happy to give your particular plan our consideration, upon
receipt of further details.

Cordially,

Answering letter

Dear Mr. Sampson,

The cost of our Tollin's Travelcade to Hawaii via jet economy class from San Francisco to Honolulu is $145.10 one way, or $290.20 round trip.

The fare via jet first class is $160.90 one way, or $321.80 round trip. Please add 5% federal transportation tax to the above fares.

We are enclosing additional literature on this new 1965 vacation in Hawaii. Please let us hear from you if you need further information.

Looking forward to welcoming you and Mrs. Sampson to the next group leaving in June, we remain,

Sincerely yours,

Incoming letter

An Interview

Dear Mr. Robbins,

I'm a 1961 graduate in business administration of Bates College. Presently, I'm working for Gates Airlines in Detroit as Passenger Service coordinator. The job is interesting and my employers seem satisfied, but company profits for 1964 have been extremely slim. The word has just gone out that certain jobs will be eliminated for 1965, in an effort to boost the profit picture for the year ahead. Unfortunately, the job of Passenger Service coordinator is on the list.

My experience and enthusiasm should prove of interest to Vanderbilt Airways. Passenger service is of prime importance to any growing airline and I'm sure that Gates will give me a favorable reference (their Personnel Manager is Mr. Joseph Howland).

Will you set aside a quarter of an hour sometime soon? I'd like to talk with you about Vanderbilt and why I think I fit into their picture. You may reach me at the above address or by phoning Collins 8-1700.

Cordially,

Answering letter

Dear Mr. Siler,

Mr. Robbins has asked me to write to tell you that he will be very happy to chat with you about your job experience and the possibility of a position with Vanderbilt Airways.

He will be free to see you on Monday the 13th at 2:00 P.M. If for any reason you cannot make it at that time, will you please phone me right away?

Cordially,

Incoming letter

An Interview

Dear Mr. Enders,

Our mutual friend, Mr. Martin Tolland, tells me you recently expressed interest in hiring an assistant to relieve you of some of the burdens and pressures of your daily work functions.

Mr. Tolland thinks that I might fill the bill and I would appreciate it very much if you will grant me an interview at your early convenience.

My job résumé is enclosed. You will note that my background is strong in the area of responsibility and that my interests are largely in the area of business administration and cost analysis.

I can be reached at the above address or by telephone and will be extremely grateful for some expression of interest from you.

Cordially,

Answering letter

Dear Mr. Roberts,

The résumé you sent me recently certainly seems to indicate that you should be well qualified for the job as assistant comptroller here at Enders, Jennison & Brown.

Will you please come in for an interview with our Personnel Manager, Miss Roberta Clark, on Tuesday, July 14th, at 1:30 P.M.? After you talk with Miss Clark, I will be glad to see you for a few moments in my office.

Cordially,

Incoming letter

An Interview

Dear Mrs. Swanson,

By phone yesterday, your secretary asked me to send in my job résumé, with the thought that perhaps there will be an opening in your merchandising department sometime soon.

The résumé is enclosed. After you've had a chance to read it, I'd appreciate it very much if you can arrange to see me for a short talk, at which time I'd like the opportunity to tell you why I think I fit into the picture at Foster and why I hope you'll give me consideration for the merchandising department position.

You can reach me by telephone at Hayley 1-1148 during the day and at Walker 7-1200 any evening after 5:30 P.M., or write me at 33 East 63rd Street, West Kansas City.

Cordially,

Answering letter

Dear Miss Gladstone,

Thank you for sending in your résumé. There will be an opening in the merchandising department in about three weeks, so I'd suggest that you come in to see me on October 23rd, at 3:00 P.M. At that time, we can discuss this position and its requirements.

Cordially,

Incoming letter

An Appointment

Dear Mr. Endicott,

I have always admired your work, particularly the way you handle dialogue. Now I have an idea for a script and the dialogue for the first two acts is already written. It seems to be the sort of a thing you do so successfully and I'd like an opportunity to discuss it and show it to you.

I'll be happy to call on you at your earliest convenience. Will you try to arrange an appointment for me in the near future?

Cordially,

Answering letter

Dear Mr. Lawton,

We are always in the market for new play ideas, and I'd like very much to talk with you.

Please call my secretary at Hobart 9-9999 for an appointment early next week. If you can make it at lunch time, we can eat right here in the cafeteria.

Cordially,

Incoming letter

An Appointment

Dear Mr. Little,

My employer Mr. Alfred Small expects to be in Dayton on Thursday, April 10th, for the entire day. He is most anxious to see you so that you may discuss the approach to be taken in the forthcoming Superior Court case on the part of McNally-Little.

Mr. Small has only one definite appointment in Dayton for the 10th and that is at 4:30 P.M., just before his departure time. Will you please drop me a note telling me at what hour and place it will be convenient for you to meet with him? He suggests lunch if that fits into your schedule.

Cordially,

Answering letter

Dear Miss Fraser,

I'm very glad that Mr. Small is coming to Dayton on Thursday, because I'm most anxious to discuss the details of the case for McNally-Little.

I will be free for lunch at 12 noon, and will come directly to the Eagle Restaurant on Main Street. Please ask Mr. Dayton to meet me there.

Cordially,

Incoming letter

To Show Designs

Dear Mr. Juneau,

The fact that you expressed interest in me when you read that I was awarded the Design Medal of the Year last February makes me wonder if that interest might not be converted into cash sales and profits for Juneau Metal Products.

I have drawn sketches for a new line of earrings which I believe would fit into your production schedule for the coming Christmas season. The designs are not only novel and in good taste, but there is also incorporated a new concept in earring stay-on-ability, which has always been a problem for the non-pierced ear.

If you'd like to see my sketches, I'll be happy to come into your office any day next week. Just name the time and day which is most convenient for you. I know the new earring design will excite you and your associates.

Cordially,

Answering letter

Dear Mr. Anthony,

Mr. Juneau has asked me to write you that he is very anxious to see the sketches you have made of your new line of earrings. He will be free on Wednesday at 1:30 P.M., and would like to see you at that time.

If this time is not convenient, please let me know right away.

Cordially,

Incoming letter

To Show Merchandise

Dear Miss Manners,

I know you are interested in early American antiques and I have something in the furniture line that I believe will delight you. It is an authentic piece and I have a written background story in connection with it.

If you'd like to see this exciting example of early Americana, I'll be happy to show it to you at my shop on Northern Boulevard in Manhasset at noon on Wednesday of next week. Because you are such an ardent collector, I will not display the piece for my other customers until I hear from you.

If noon on Wednesday is not convenient, just drop me a note suggesting another time earlier in the week. If I do not hear from you, I'll assume that you'll keep our appointment on Wednesday.

Cordially,

Answering letter

Dear Mr. Edwards,

Thank you for being so thoughtful and remembering that I'm always interested in early American antiques.

I will be at your shop at noon on Tuesday, since I've already made other plans for Wednesday.

Cordially,

Incoming letter

To Show Merchandise

Dear Dr. Marion,

I shall be in Newark on Monday, February 3rd, and would like very much to see you that morning, if it is convenient. I have an entirely new line of dental materials to show you and I know you'll be interested in hearing all about them.

If ten o'clock on Monday morning is satisfactory, I'll be at your office at that time. If another hour would be better, just ask your secretary to let me know, please.

Cordially,

Answering letter

Dear Mr. Greene,

Thank you for your letter of the 13th. I know that Dr. Marion would be very interested in seeing your new line of dental materials, but he will not be in the office all next week.

Could you plan to come in two weeks from Monday at 10:00 A.M.? Please let me know right away so that I can fit you into the morning schedule.

Cordially,

Incoming letter

Second Request to Correct Error

Dear Bob,

Here we go again! Jack Dailey sent the enclosed invoice to me for obvious reasons. I'm sure you'll recall our conversations regarding the erroneous billing of this account. I had told Jack that you assured me it would be wiped off the books, but then he received the enclosed.

I would greatly appreciate it if you'd instruct the Billing Department to issue a credit memo at once. Also, in order to put Jack's mind at rest, will you please write him directly telling him he can ignore this invoice? Thanks very much.

Cordially,

Answering letter

Dear Tom,

Of course I remember our discussion of Jack Dailey's billing. And I did issue instructions to cancel the invoice. However, something went haywire along the line and we owe you and Jack an apology. Attached is a copy of my second memo, written this morning. I'm sure there'll be no further problem.

Also enclosed is a carbon copy of my note to Jack Dailey. Thanks very much for calling the matter to my attention so promptly.

Cordially,

Incoming letter

For Further Information

Dear Mr. Thompson,

The sales training correspondence course offered through your ads sounds like an excellent idea and your organization is certainly to be commended for having taken this progressive step forward. I don't know whether we will be able to offer this course to any of our franchised dealers, but I understand the matter is being considered by our sales department.

In the meantime, I'd appreciate it if you will put us on your mailing list for this course, if you can do so on a no-charge basis. I shall continue to recommend our participation in this project.

Cordially,

Answering letter

Dear Mr. Schrader,

We are very happy to put you on our mailing lists so that you will receive future installments of our sales training correspondence course. We are enclosing Lesson Number I with this letter. Will you please pass it along to your sales department, as I am sure they will find it extremely helpful and interesting?

If there is any other information you need about the course at this time, please get in touch with me right away.

Cordially,

Incoming letter

A Service

Gentlemen,

We have just signed a lease for occupancy of the 11th floor of the Pelham National Bank Building on Hartford Avenue. Our occupancy begins on February 1st and we shall appreciate anything you can do to give us full telephone service by that date.

We shall need seven stationary phone positions, each with intercommunication as well as outside operator service. All of the instruments should be black and should include a "hold" button, if possible.

The janitor of the building has been authorized to give you the keys to our 11th floor suite any time after next Sunday. I have chalk-marked with an "X" each location, and would appreciate it very much if you will examine the situation and make the necessary arrangements for installation as soon as possible.

For credit references, you may check with the Pelham National Bank in the same building, as well as with the Savings and Loan Division of the Mount Vernon Mutual.

If there are any questions, you may reach me at Lehigh 5-1400. Your prompt attention will be greatly appreciated.

Cordially,

Answering letter

Dear Mr. Carroll,

Thank you for your letter of the 12th about installing telephone service in your new offices in the Pelham National Bank building.

We are sending our District Manager, Mr. Ralph Jones, along with a service man, to the building on Friday at 1:00 P.M., to go over the installation requirements as you have requested them in your letter. Will you please have someone at the building to let them in and also to answer any further questions they may have to ask? If this date is not convenient, please contact me right away, to make other arrangements.

Cordially,

Incoming letter

A Service

Dear Mr. Dupont,

Enclosed is my check for $1000, which I should like you to hold in escrow until you can fulfill my option to buy 20 shares of Consolidated American common stock at not more than $50 per share.

If you will notify me when this purchase has been made and invoice me for your usual brokerage fees, I will appreciate it very much. The stock should be purchased in my name as it appears on this letterhead, but my home address should appear on the certificate. It is 2313 Marble Road, Larchmont, New York.

Cordially,

Answering letter

Dear Mr. Kitteridge,

Thank you for your order to buy 20 shares of Consolidated American common stock, and your check for $1000 to cover the transaction.

We were able to make an advantageous buy yesterday at $48 per share. The invoice for brokerage fees and your certificate will be sent within the next few days.

Cordially,

Incoming letter

A Service

Dear Mr. Sills,

We are completely sold out on litter boxes and would appreciate it very much if you will rush to us three more cases of the $4.95 model in assorted plastic. Air express will reach us fast and, in this particular instance, we will be happy to pay the additional shipping expense.

Also, some time soon, will you send me your 1965 catalog? My inventory on many items is low due to an exceptionally heavy Christmas season. I need to reorder some of these before the end of the month.

Please write me the waybill number and date of shipment on my litter box order so that we may arrange to pick them up at the local deposit depot.

Cordially,

Answering letter

Dear Mr. Wilson,

Thank you for your order for three cases of litter boxes. With this letter we are enclosing your copy of the waybill No. 2400, for the shipment which will go from our warehouse to American Airlines tomorrow morning, the 12th of June.

Our 1965 catalog is being sent separately.

Cordially,

Incoming letter

Confirm Enrollment of Student

Dear Parents,

We are presently processing an unprecedented number of applications for the admission of new students for next year, and in order to know how many of them we can approve, we must again resort to our custom of requesting parents of present students to announce their school plans for the coming school year.

If you intend to re-enroll your son for the coming school year, please sign and return the enclosed reservation form with the reservation fee before April 1st.

This fee will be credited on the first semester's tuition

statement, or it will be refunded in the cases of those students whose withdrawal is requested by this faculty in June for unsatisfactory scholastic achievement or for poor citizenship records.

Sincerely,

Answering letter

Dear Sirs,

Thank you very much for your letter of the 14th. I have filled in the necessary information on the reservation form and am returning it with this letter, along with the reservation fee.

Sincerely,

Incoming letter

To Make a Decision

Dear Mr. Manet,

Off the record, can you tell me how you feel about the SPCA's present drive? I'm asking this because within a few days your name will be put into the hat for nomination as chairman.

If I properly recall your remark made two months ago, I was left with the distinct feeling you were not in support of this particular movement. If that is so, you need not make your position public unless you care to, but I can save you the embarrassment of turning down the nomination if I know just how you feel.

Nomination day is Tuesday, the 15th. Please drop me a line before that date.

Cordially,

Answering letter

Dear Mr. Southington,

You have a good memory: I am not in favor of the movement, so please do not put my name in for the nomination for chairman.

Thank you just the same for thinking of me. I certainly appreciate your thoughtfulness in this matter.

Cordially,

XVII

Letters OF REFUSAL

Probably the reason we joke about "yes-men" is that all of us know how much more difficult it is to say "no." But the skilled letter-writer is able to say it firmly enough, in a fashion that retains good will and helps the recipient of the letter to understand the reasons for the negative response.

Under most circumstances, the letter of refusal requires more careful thought and planning than any other type of business letter. There can be possibly nothing more important in business than to keep a customer happy and there are ways to do it even when refusing to do what he asks of you.

CHECK LIST
FOR LETTERS OF REFUSAL

1. Thank the writer for *something*.
2. Detail reasons why you must disappoint him.

3. Say "no," after conditioning him.

4. Offer substitute service or try to compromise.

Incoming letter

Contributions

Dear Mr. McIntosh,

The Maintenance Department of Lowry Hospital needs your help. This is the department which takes charge of the hospital building and its contents, the department which is entrusted with the responsibility for upkeep, repair, and furnishing of the hospital.

Lowry, as you probably know, is a 200-bed hospital. Perhaps, though, it will surprise you to know that 162 of those beds were purchased in 1937 and are still being used. If we don't replace them soon, they'll fall apart.

A good hospital bed—one which is comfortable, mobile and durable—costs $300. We know we can't possibly buy all that we need in a single year. However, by replacing 35 each year, we can see that it is possible to do the job in a five-year period. This means that we must campaign for $105,000 each year, just for the replacement of beds.

Won't you do your best to help us? Contributions are so badly needed. The enclosed envelope will make it easy to put your donation into the mail without delay. Thanks from the bottom of our hearts for your assistance.

Cordially,

Answering letter

Dear Mr. Hammond,

Thanks for your recent letter which was directed to the attention of our treasurer. After careful consideration, he asks that I explain to you that in a company like ours, with 50 divisions throughout the country, it's impossible to support the very worthwhile cause of hospitals in each of these areas. Instead, each year the corporation contributes to the Federated National Hospital Fund.

Therefore, I'm sorry to tell you we will be unable to contribute locally to this fine project, with which we wish you the greatest success.

Cordially,

Incoming letter

Dear Mr. Pendergast,

I learned with pleasure today that you will be stopping off in Manchester on or about November 17th.

Since that is the week a committee here will meet to talk of our bicentennial celebration, I wonder if it would fit into your plans to join a group of our townspeople for a discussion of the bicentennial parade which you staged for the Township of Rye last summer.

Many of the ideas which you used in Rye can, I am sure, be applied to our own celebration next spring. Your own affair was such a remarkable success and you were so instrumental in its planning that I am sure our committee would welcome the opportunity to ply you with questions, and to hear your advice.

We should so much appreciate getting together with you.

Cordially,

Answering letter

A Committee Meeting

Dear Mr. Duluth,

The opportunity to talk with your committee and to "blow my horn" a little about the success of the Rye bicentennial celebration last spring sounds extremely attractive to me.

Unfortunately, however, my stay in Manchester will be limited to a single morning, during which time I must devote myself entirely to the purpose of my trip, which is to address the personnel at our branch office there.

I do thank you, though, for your kind invitation and wish you every success with the forthcoming celebration.

Cordially,

Incoming letter

Dear Mr. Greene,

The Town Selectmen's Committee will meet at the Town House Grill for luncheon on April 3rd, at 12:30 P.M. The purpose of the meeting is to organize a campaign to promote zoning regulations in our town. Since you have shown interest and expressed yourself in favor of this project, we would like very much to have you join us for further discussion.

Will you let us know right away if you can be with us?

Cordially,

Answering letter

A Committee Meeting

Dear Mr. Brown,

Thank you very much for your invitation to join the Town Selectmen's Committee at luncheon on April 3rd.

A previous commitment makes it impossible for me to attend. Since I cannot be present, perhaps you will be kind enough to convey to the committee my promise of support in their campaign to establish zoning regulations for our fair city.

Cordially,

Incoming letter

Dear Mr. Limon,

In response to the advertisement you ran in last night's *Eagle* in the Help Wanted column, I am sending my résumé and would very much like to have my application considered for the job as Personnel Manager.

My present job is only part time and I would be able to come in any morning you wish for an interview. Will you please let me know when it will be convenient for you to see me?

Cordially,

Answering letter

An Interview

Dear Miss Mullen,

Thank you very much for your letter of the 23rd.

I wish I could tell you to come right in for an interview. However, your job résumé makes it clear that you are really not quite ready at this time for a job which entails so much responsibility. It usually takes a number of years of experience to prepare one for the heavy-duty functions of a personnel manager for an organization the size of Peerless.

My suggestion to you is that you continue with the courses you are now taking at night school and that you attempt to find a job as assistant to a personnel manager in some smaller company. Later on, if you are still interested in the Peerless Company, you might come in and fill out one of our application forms so that the next time there's a managerial opening, your name will be considered.

I wish you the very best of success in your career.

Cordially,

Incoming letter

An Interview

Dear Andrew,

Our friendship is extremely important to me so I hope it will not suffer when I tell you I cannot arrange for an interview here at this particular time.

I still believe your background and ability are right for a job of these proportions, but I am not in charge of Personnel, and our Personnel Manager feels she has found someone with more experience and more proper qualifications for the position.

Believe me when I say I will keep trying. But meanwhile, don't stand still. Why not write to a few of the smaller companies to see if any one of them has an opening? Then, when something develops here, you will have added extra and valuable experience to your job abilities.

With very kindest personal regards, I am

Cordially,

Answering letter

Dear Dick,

Thank you very much for your letter about the job opening. I want you to know that I understand your position and since you had to be the one to tell me I'm not quite ready for the job, I can assure you that our friendship will not suffer for it but will grow stronger.

You gave me a bit of excellent advice which I'm going to follow. First, however, I have to ask a favor of you. Will you send me a list of smaller companies where a job such as I'm looking for might be available now or in the near future?

Cordially,

Incoming letter

Dear Mr. Howard,

It is my great pleasure to inform you that on Tuesday, April 14th, at our monthly seminar, it was decided unanimously to award you the Silver Medal for your recent contribution in your research work on the bubble fish. Your courage and initiative in experimenting with this kind of food is highly commendable and we are pleased, indeed, that you have received proper recognition.

Please accept our sincere congratulations and hope for your continued success.

Cordially,

Answering letter

A Proffered Honor

Gentlemen,

In the year 1931, the Scottish Marine Research Society published a book on the edibility of the bubble fish. It was written by Jefferson Andrews, a marine explorer, who died in Scotland late last year. Very little attention was paid to this revelation at the time the book appeared, especially here in America, but I obtained a copy and referred to it quite often in my own experimental work. Hence, I think you will understand why I do not feel that I am entitled to the award you so kindly proffer and cannot accept the Silver Medal.

While I cannot accept the award, I do want you to know how pleased I am that my further experimentation has been observed by both you and the press. The bubble fish can be a partial answer to the world's need for easily obtainable food to nurture the many over-populated countries of the world, many of which are on the brink of starvation.

Thank you very much again for your kindness.

Sincerely,

Incoming letter

Dear Mr. Bunch,

You can help our Party now—when your help really counts.

Your name has been given by your local committee with the suggestion that we ask you for a statement in support of Mr. Benjamin Dawes who is a candidate for the House of Representatives from the State of Florida.

Our Party has a program that can restore good government to America. We know Mr. Dawes will continue to win issues of importance to you, personally, and to the nation as a whole.

Your statement by return mail will be appreciated.

Cordially,

Answering letter

A Political Candidate

Dear Mr. Smith,

Thank you for your letter of February 15th requesting a statement from me in favor of the candidacy of Mr. Benjamin Dawes for Congressman from the State of Florida.

To be perfectly frank with you, I am still uncertain that I shall vote for Mr. Dawes and need more time to make up my mind about the several candidates whose hats are in the ring. And should I decide not to cast my vote in Mr. Dawes' direction, this does not mean that I look upon him unfavorably as a person. It will simply mean that I like somebody else's platform better.

As a matter of fact, I've known Mr. Dawes for a long time and am sure that he would agree with my decision not to endorse him publicly until I am definite about my own vote.

Why don't you get back to me in another month or two? After I've heard other candidates and studied what they have to offer, I may be able to give you the statement you want.

Cordially,

XVIII

Letters OF COLLECTION

AND CREDIT

Nearly all human beings are pretty touchy about the state of their finances and since business organizations are not only made up of human beings but also depend upon their financial reputation for survival, this touchiness carries over into the business world.

Large companies usually have departments made up of persons skilled in matters of collection and credit. Smaller ones and individual employers may expect the secretary to learn this skill. Perhaps the most important thing to remember when dealing with such situations is that the good will of the customer or recipient of the letter *must be retained*. Therefore, it's important to blame the lack of payment on an intangible or an understandable and excusable circumstance. Actually, the good collection letter *excuses* the delinquent, while pressing for payment.

CHECK LIST

FOR LETTERS OF COLLECTION AND CREDIT

1. Remind that payment is due or overdue.
2. Excuse the "oversight."
3. Ask for prompt payment to avoid the consequence of a poor credit rating.
4. Thank in advance for the forthcoming payment.
5. Hint at the unhappy consequences.

Incoming letter

Dear Sirs,

In order to complete arrangements for a charge account at Denton's I have filled out the preliminary forms and am returning them with this letter. Will you send along my Charga-Plate as quickly as possible? I'll be making a trip into the city soon, and will probably want to make some purchases at Denton's.

Cordially,

Answering letter

Arrangements for Charge Account

Dear Mr. Neff,

We are pleased to send you the enclosed Charga-Plate issued in accordance with your instructions.

Will you please sign the Charga-Plate in ink immediately? The signature should be that of the person who will use the plate when making purchases.

Also, will you be kind enough to mark off the enclosed form, indicating whether you wish to be billed on a monthly calendar basis with a 30-day charge without interest on any item available, or would you prefer our budget plan which bills you for 10 percent of your outstanding balance each month? The interest on the budget plan is 1 percent a month on the balance as it appears on billing date.

Thank you very much for shopping at Denton's.

Cordially,

Incoming letter

Reminder of Payment Overdue

THERE'S A VERY GOOD CHANCE, *Mr. Jones,*

that by the time this reaches you, your account will have been settled in full. If so, please don't read any further.

However, I've noticed that as of this writing we haven't received payment on the very small amount still outstanding on your account.

Was there something wrong with the merchandise we delivered you, Mr. Jones? Or was there some question about the bill itself?

Whatever the reason, I wish you'd drop me a line and tell me frankly. Once I understand the problem, I'll do everything possible to make the necessary adjustments.

If you simply forgot about the bill (and who doesn't do this once in a while?), just attach your check or money order to this letter and return it to me in the next mail. There's a postpaid envelope enclosed for your convenience.

Cordially,

Answering letter

Dear Sirs,

Thank you for your patience about my account. There is nothing wrong with your merchandise and there is no question about the bill. It has all been my fault.

About two months ago, my company suddenly rushed me off to the Far East on a research story—and I simply flew away. In the meantime there was no one to carry on my personal affairs.

Enclosed is my check to cover the amount mentioned in your letter.

Cordially,

Incoming letter

Threatened Loss of Credit

Gentlemen,

Your account as shown on the enclosed statement is, to be very honest with you, quite puzzling to me as a credit manager.

Our Sales Department evidently thinks you are a solid enough corporation to continue selling you merchandise even though two of the items shown on the enclosed statement are long past due. On the face of it, your credit standing with us will be in very poor shape, especially because of the March 1st item ($470.00).

Though I have written you several times about the account, I have not had the courtesy of a reply and am wondering just why, after extending you credit as we have, you have not seen fit to answer my letters.

When we add the August billing to the items shown on the enclosed statement, the balance on your account will be very close to $5,000 and we must now call a halt to any further purchasing until the balance shown on the enclosed statement ($3,460.00) is paid. We dislike very much doing business in this manner but you leave us no choice.

Cordially,

Answering letter

Dear Mr. Bauer,

I must confess that I have had some difficulty in paying the amount owing you since March 1st, primarily because we have had a strike here which ended only two weeks ago.

I've checked with our accounting department, and find that I can now pay all of the March 1st item and a good portion of the balance due you up to August 1st. A check will be sent you tomorrow.

I'm sure now that we have our union problems settled and production is again going full steam ahead, we'll be able to pay our bills as they become due.

I'm extremely sorry for the inconvenience caused you.

Cordially,

Incoming letter

Threatened Loss of Credit

Dear Mrs. Manning,

The holiday season is so busy for all of us that sometimes we overlook things that should get our attention. That is probably the case where our bill for your carpets is concerned.

However, our Credit Manager has asked me to remind you that unless we receive a check from you by Monday afternoon, we'll have to reclaim the carpeting. That means, of course, that not only will you be subject to embarrassment, but also that we will have to turn your name over to our attorney and you will find it very difficult to get credit elsewhere should you so desire.

Please attend to this matter at once. The carpeting looked

so lovely in your home that I should hate to see you deprived of it, not to mention the fact that I should not like to take such extreme measures when they can so easily be avoided.

Very truly yours,

Answering letter

Dear Mr. Freed,

Your letter of the 12th came as something of a shock. I find after going over my checkbook that I paid my bill a month ago. Since apparently the check was lost in the mail, I have stopped payment as of this morning and am enclosing a replacement check for the amount in full.

Sincerely,

Incoming letter

Payment Long Overdue

Dear Gerry,

I don't like to dun you, but it has now become urgent that you forward your check for $200 as soon as you receive this letter.

I think we've been more patient than most on this matter, and you will recall that I delivered the merchandise to you on a 30-day payment arrangement. Our invoice is now more than 120 days old and you have apparently ignored our statements.

If this has just slipped your mind, Gerry, please get your check into the mail today. If there are other problems, at least drop me a line and explain your position. If we don't hear from you by the 15th, we shall have to put this matter into the hands of our attorneys. I don't want to do that.

Cordially,

Answering letter

Dear Bob,

I well realize that I have put you in something of a "spot" since I have been unable to pay the $200 even after the 30-day arrangement. Now, I'm glad to tell you that one of my clients has paid up and so a good part of the money received here was sent by check to you in yesterday's mail.

The balance will be sent along next week. Thanks so much for your patience.

Cordially,

Incoming letter

Bills Overdue—Plan for Payment

Dear Sirs,

Enclosed is our July 1st statement carrying a notation that no further purchases can be delivered to your company until we receive full payment of our March and June billings.

When we accepted the order for merchandise delivered in June, we assumed that the small balance still on our books at that time for your March purchases would be paid without delay. Unfortunately, this was not the case and ordinarily we would be considering taking legal action on a billing as old as the March item shown on the enclosed statement.

In view of what we can find out about your firm from a credit standpoint, it's a little difficult to understand why the $740 has been on our books since last March.

We have always tried to settle our collection difficulties in a friendly manner and, therefore, sincerely hope that by next Thursday, July 13, we will have a check for at least the March invoice, and that by the end of July we will have your check taking care of the June bill.

Very truly yours,

Answering letter

Dear Mr. Jennings,

I'm very glad to say that I'm finally in a position to pay in full for the March and June billings. My check for the full amount is enclosed.

Cordially,

Incoming letter

Memo to John Smith

Re: Mr. Ashford

John, the attached invoice is so far overdue that we cannot extend further credit on Mr. Ashford's account. Can you see if he will respond to a letter from you? Thanks very much.

Try to Keep Credit Rating

Answering letter

Dear Mr. Ashford,

Our Billing Department has just passed along to me the attached invoice with a notation that we "cannot extend further credit on this account."

Since I am a lot closer to you than our Billing Department, it occurs to me that this delinquency is simply the result of the vacation season. I know how short-handed we get during the summer months when there are always at least three or four of our employees out of the office, and I'm sure that happens in your organization, too.

Is it possible that the last two invoices are under the pile on your desk? If you could find time to dig them out and pass them along for prompt payment, I can ask the Credit Department to reinstate your credit position. Will you let me know about this right away please, Mr. Ashford?

Cordially,

Incoming letter

A Misunderstanding

Dear Mr. Parent,

The Dickerman advertising agency returned our statement showing a $60.98 charge as of May 29th. A note on the statement reads "Returning for you to cancel as per instructions of A. Parent."

Will you please explain to me this rather peculiar situation? Usually, when you recommend the cancellation of a charge we receive written notification from you.

What are we to do? Do you wish this charge cancelled or is there some misunderstanding on the part of our client?

Cordially,

Answering letter

Dear Mr. Dolby,

Our records show that we wrote Mr. Dickerman right after the 1st indicating that we would have to make an adjustment in the billing. A copy of this letter was sent to your office. Something must have happened to it.

This was not a cancellation, as Mr. Dickerman seems to

believe, but an adjustment of the cost. Please hold everything until I have another discussion about this with him.

Cordially,

Incoming letter

Offer of Payment Plan

Dear Mr. Morrison,

Absence is said to make the heart grow fonder—and I guess it's true. For example, we miss your business, and wonder why you haven't used your charge account in recent months.

If it's because of that small outstanding sum you owe us, Mr. Morrison, that shouldn't prove a hindrance. Even though, through some oversight, you haven't yet paid your September bill of $43.50, we hope you're not doing your shopping elsewhere.

If it would be more convenient, you may pay off the bill at the rate of only $14.50 a month over a period of three months. The carrying charges will amount to only 43 cents a month, which can be added to each month's payment.

Come on in and start your Christmas shopping, Mr. Morrison. Just stop at the credit desk on the eighth floor and make your first small payment on that bill. Then use your charge account, as usual, for additional purchases.

We hope to see you very soon again.

Cordially,

Answering letter

Dear Mr. Boynton,

Let me compliment you on your very considerate letter of the 4th. I have had a serious illness and death in my family, and many things have been neglected during this time. Now that I am finally able to take care of my personal affairs—the first item on the list is to pay bills.

Enclosed is my check for $43.50 to cover the full amount due. I'm sorry this payment is so late.

Cordially,

Incoming letter

Dear Mr. Pearson,

I'm at a loss to know why I can't make your Credit Manager, Mr. Dexter, understand my problem. I have not paid my bill for the October shipment because the bill was for twice as much merchandise as I received. Someone made an error along the way, and Mr. Dexter doesn't seem to want to do anything about it.

Now, I have another shipment on the way. I hope I won't be billed double for that, too. Can you find a way to help clear up this problem, Mr. Pearson?

Cordially,

Answering letter

Corrected Billing

Dear Miss Deusen,

To answer your letter of last Monday: the invoice you will receive for the merchandise shipped you on December 8th will be for only one-half of the regular price, or $92.50, under an arrangement made with our Credit Manager, Mr. Dexter, because of an error made in the previous shipment.

I hope this arrangement will be satisfactory to you, Miss Deusen.

Cordially,

Incoming letter

Dear Mr. Kennedy,

We have just received a large order from the Miehle Sales Corporation of Omaha, Nebraska with a request that we extend the usual credit terms. Your company name was given as a credit reference so I would appreciate it very much if you will give me your recommendations for the extension of such credit, based on your experience with the Miehle organization this past year.

Your cooperation will be very gratefully received and you may rest assured that your recommendation will be held in the strictest confidence.

Cordially,

Answering letter

Good Credit Reference

Dear Mr. Francis,

Our Credit Department tells me that our experience with the Miehle Sales Corporation has been excellent. The company pays within 30 days, and we have billed out a very healthy amount in this fashion since the time of their first order which was in early 1961.

On the strength of these facts, I feel you will be well justified to extend a reasonable amount of credit to the people at Miehle.

Do call on me again if I can be helpful.

Cordially,

Incoming letter

Dear Alfred,

We're having some trouble collecting from Smithers-Ronaldi Company. Will you please, at your earliest convenience, give me a *Dun and Bradstreet* report on them?

Thanks very much.

Cordially,

Answering letter

Poor Credit Rating

Dear Moe,

Enclosed is the *Dun and Bradstreet* report on Smithers-Ronaldi Company requested by you last week.

After reading this, Moe, I don't believe we should let them run up any further bills. In other words, if they don't pay the February charge promptly, I think we should refuse further deliveries. Their Cash and Accounts Receivables are far overshadowed by their Accounts Payables, loans, etc. Best regards.

Cordially,

XIX

Letters OF ANNOUNCEMENT

𝕍? Often, the announcement of the appointment of a new employee, a merger, a new price schedule, a new policy or a change of address is sent out in the form of a news release. Such releases follow a standard format which requires that they be brief, yet include the answers to the newspaper reporter's queries: *who? what? when? where?* and *why?*

On occasion, in lieu of a news release, individual letters are written announcing something of importance.

CHECK LIST
FOR LETTERS OF ANNOUNCEMENT

1. Make the announcement at once.
2. Be specific about time, dates, titles, company name and address, etc.
3. Elaborate with background material to add importance to the announcement.

Incoming letter

Retirement

Dear Mr. Maloney,

Like most of our customers, you probably know that on January 1st, Mr. William Maguire, your long-time contact, will retire from his vice-presidency of The Taconic Supply Company.

Mr. Maguire has been with The Taconic Supply Company for 31 years and his friends in the trade are many and loyal. He has most certainly earned the right to a more leisurely way of life, but his smiling face and helpful manner will be sorely missed by those he has called on these many years.

He has asked me to tell you, however, that he is completely confident that your needs will be served most adequately by his successor, Mr. Daniel Thorpe, whose background in the supply business covers more than 12 years. Mr. Thorpe will stop in to introduce himself right after the first of the year.

Cordially,

Answering letter

Dear Mr. Haggerty,

I hope you'll pass along to Mr. Maguire our good wishes for his future happiness. We'll miss him and his service very much.

Since I am going away on a business trip for about 10 weeks, I won't be here in my office until about February 10th. Please have Mr. Thorpe delay his visit until the middle of February at which time I'll be happy to see him.

Cordially,

Incoming letter

Dear Mr. Eddy,

It seems very strange to me that letters to your organization are being returned marked "Moved, no forwarding address." I know that we haven't done any business with you for the past six months. Have you really moved? If so, shouldn't you let us know where we can find you?

Cordially,

Answering letter

New Location

Dear Mr. Monroe,

Yes, we moved to a new location on August 1st, a location more in keeping with the prestige and importance the Ganz Company has attained in the past few years. In addition, the new site will make it easier to call on us, since it's convenient to bus and subway lines, not to mention the fact that we'll have our own 300-car parking lot in the rear of the building.

Why not drop in sometime right after the 15th of August and let us give you the grand tour? Naturally, we'll be proud to show you around and you'll probably be interested in the new computer system we're having installed.

Cordially,

Incoming letter

Expansion of Business—New Location

 Associates, *Inc.* 1845 Post Road, Warwick, Rhode Island,   Tel. 739-4900
MARKETING   Tel. 739-4901
ADVERTISING   Tel. 739-4902
PUBLIC RELATIONS   Tel. 739-4903

Mr. David Williams
Marketing Services, Inc.
31 Canal Street
Providence, R.I.

Dear Mr. Williams:

In our 21st month of operation we are proud to announce that
our company has grown to the extent where new and larger quarters
have become necessary.

Our new location is in the Airport Professional Building just
completed at 1845 Post Road in Warwick, R.I.

We will occupy 2,500 square feet on one floor of this 2 story
ultra-modern, air-conditioned office building overlooking the new
R.I. state airport terminal.

On behalf of all of us at Spencer-Claire, I want to thank you
for the confidence you have shown in our efforts without which this
growth would not have been possible.

Please accept this personal invitation to visit us in our new
quarters to see for yourself the most modern, most productive
working area of any firm in our business.

Sincerely,

SPENCER-CLAIRE ASSOCIATES, INC.

Sheldon D. Spencer
President

Answering letter

Dear Mr. Spencer,

It has been a pleasure to do business with Spencer-Claire Associates, Inc., for the past 15 years. I want to congratulate you on your success and growth to the extent that you are now in new and larger quarters.

I plan to be in your vicinity in the very near future and will, of course, be happy to drop in for a chat and to see your new working area.

Cordially,

Incoming letter

Dear Mr. Hammond,

Since the first of the year we've had to make so many phone calls to your plant and it has become so expensive that I'm wondering how we can continue to do business with you.

Isn't it possible for you people to set up an *Enterprise* number as a service for your customers in the middle and far west?

Cordially,

Answering letter

New Communications System

Dear Mr. Smith,

In reply to your letter of November 15th, your suggestion is much appreciated and we are acting on it at once.

Effective as of January 1st, you may reach us at our

home office in Buffalo simply by dialing the operator and asking for Enterprise 6654.

There is, of course, no charge for these calls. I hope this will prove to be a service which contributes to our efficiency and promptness when doing business with your organization.

Cordially,

Incoming letter

Dear Mr. Harrison,

Now that I'm a stockholder, (I just purchased 20 shares) I'd like to know more about the Eldridge Company, its background and its products. Can you send along such information?

Cordially,

Answering letter

To New Stockholders

Dear Friend,

Thank you very much for your recent purchase of Eldridge common stock.

As a new stockholder, you will be interested in some facts about the company of which you are now part owner.

The Eldridge Company was founded in 1922, beginning as a small shop in Brooklyn, New York. Through steady growth, the Company progressed to increasingly larger facilities, all in Brooklyn, until the recent purchase of the present building at 145-005 Thirty-Ninth Avenue, in late 1962. The Company has been publicly owned since April, 1960.

The Eldridge Company is engaged in the design, production and distribution of electronic equipment, primarily for the testing and measuring fields. It is a major producer of such equipment. Eldridge products are marketed not only in the United States but in every major market throughout the world.

Sales volume in 1963 was approximately $7,000,000. Exact figures will be released shortly when our annual statement becomes available.

If you'd like to visit Eldridge and tour the most modern such plant in existence, just contact me by letter and I'll be happy to arrange such a tour.

Cordially,

Incoming letter

Dear Mr. Flanagan,

In making up our next year's budget, we are very anxious to know if you anticipate any increase in advertising rates.

Will you please let us know at your earliest convenience? Thank you very much.

Cordially,

Answering letter

Advertising Rate Increase

Dear Mr. Merrick,

Effective on September 1, 1965, there will be a slight increase in advertising rates necessitated by a continuing rise in costs all along the line.

The new one-time black-and-white full page rate will

be $700, with corresponding adjustments in other size space units. A copy of Rate Card No. 7 detailing these changes is enclosed.

I am happy to tell you, however, that this modest increase will be very largely offset by an increase in circulation, since the new advertising rate will be based on 50,000 net paid, also effective with September. This will pay off for advertisers in additional response to their advertising messages. It will continue to make *Hotel Magazine* the most effective advertising medium in the field.

Cordially,

Incoming letter

New Salesman

Dear Mr. Agnew,

It's with pleasure that I write this letter to tell you that, effective January 1, 1966, Mr. Edward Means will join our sales staff. Mr. Means comes from a background of sales and promotion, and his most recent connection was with the Madison Insurance Company. He's an extremely personable man, as well as a capable and knowledgeable one. He'll be calling you for an appointment in early January and has some interesting ideas I'd like him to present to you.

I know I can count on you to give him your usual hearty welcome.

Cordially,

Answering letter

Dear Mr. Conrad,

Thank you for letting me know about your new man, Mr. Edward Means. I'll be very happy to see him and to discuss with him the new ideas you mentioned.

Please have him phone my secretary to make a definite appointment.

Cordially,

Incoming letter

A Merger

Dear Mr. Fleury,

Effective on January 1, 1964, the Stetson Company will become a subsidiary of the well-known organization, Lancet and Fears. This merger gives added strength to Stetson both in terms of public acceptance and operating capital, meaning that we can serve you more promptly, more efficiently and more thoroughly than ever before in our history.

I'm sure you'll be pleased that all of your old friends at Stetson will remain on the staff since the new owners have understandably recognized the ability and true worth of those with whom you have been doing business for the past 10 years.

Cordially,

Answering letter

Dear Mr. Stetson,

Congratulations on your merger with Lancet and Fears. I know it is a great move for both companies and I wish you continued success and prosperity.

Cordially,

Incoming letter

Dear Mr. Syer,

Please reserve one-page space for our advertising in each of the first three issues of the Carnegie Hall Program. We are somewhat puzzled about how the billing will be handled. Can you explain, please?

Cordially,

Answering letter

Advertising in New Publication

THE CARNEGIE
HALL PROGRAM

Advertising and Executive Offices: Great Barrington, Mass. Phone 1300 / from New York, WA 5-2863

WARREN B. SYER
Publisher

To All Carnegie Hall Program Advertisers

As you probably know we have guaranteed all full season advertisers a minimum of 250 events. Also 5 and 3 month advertisers are guaranteed a minimum of 125 and 65 events respectively. For the sanity of your accounting department (as well as ours) we will invoice 10 times a year - on or about the first of October through the first of July. It is impossible to predict in advance just how many events will occur in a given month. Therefore each invoice will be accompanied by ad tear sheets that will vary widely in number. At this writing it looks like less than ten events in September, for example, though you will receive a full month's invoice on or about October first for September advertising. Please don't be alarmed by this. Everyone is assured the full measure of events for which they have paid. All advertising will run - no matter how many months are involved - until the guaranteed number of events have taken place. Here's an example:

A three month advertiser - starting in September - will receive bills October 1, November 1 and December 1. The first invoice might be accompanied by 8 program tear sheets, the second by 22 and the third by 25. This would total 55 - 10 short of the guarantee. In such a situation the advertising will be run again in December - and a "no balance due" invoice rendered on January 1 with perhaps 25 more tear sheets - bringing the actual number of programed events delivered to 80. The same example can be followed through for 5 month and full-season advertisers, of course.

Therefore - everyone will get at least their minimum number of programs - and in most cases a bonus. Another proof that your decision to advertise in the all-new CARNEGIE HALL PROGRAM was a wise one.

If you have any questions - please drop me a line.

Sincerely,

/ah

A DIVISION OF HIGH FIDELITY MAGAZINE

XX

Letters OF INVITATION

❦ Whether your employer or the company for which you work is planning a sales meeting, a management seminar, an industry cocktail party or dinner or any get-together where invitations will be issued, it's important to determine in advance whether the occasion can be characterized as formal or informal. If formality is to be the rule, the decision will probably be to send out engraved or quasi-engraved invitations. A good book of etiquette will tell you how to word them, or answer them.

However, most business invitations can be classified as informal. The degree to which the informality is carried out will determine the type of invitation to be written. This can vary considerably, running the gamut from the gay, lighthearted poster type of invitation with original art to the warm and friendly personal letter. Important to remember is the fact that all invitations must indicate the time and place of the gathering, the character of the party—dinner, cocktails, lunch, dance, lecture, etc.—and, if a reply is required, mention of this.

CHECK LIST
FOR LETTERS OF INVITATION

1. Tell why the event is taking place: to honor someone, to introduce someone, to set off a campaign, and so on.
2. Tell when and where, and whether dinner, lunch, etc.
3. Give specific hours for arrival and departure, where important.
4. Ask for an acceptance or refusal by a given date.

Incoming letter

To All Employees—End-of-Year Party

It's been a good year at Metropolis, a year of successful sales and better-than-anticipated profits—and each and every one of you has contributed to this fine record of achievement. We've tried, as is our practice, to show our appreciation through normal methods—your pay envelopes. But such an outstanding year deserves a more physical celebration, and we've decided that a party is in order.

The date is Friday, November 22, at 6:30 P.M. The place—the Blue Grotto on State Street. Cocktails will be served from 6:30 to 7:30. Then a good dinner is on the schedule. Afterward, it's to be dancing until dawn with music by the city's best known orchestra, Leo Donelan. We want you to bring a guest—your wife or husband if you're married, a boy or girl friend if you're single. It's on the house and we hope to have a spectacular time!

In order to make proper reservations, will you send your memo of acceptance or refusal to the attention of Jenny Conover in the Personnel Department, no later than Monday, November 19th?

Cordially,

Answering letter

Dear Miss Conover,

Mrs. Thompson and I will be delighted to attend the Metropolis party at the Blue Grotto on November 22, at 6:30 P.M. Thank you very much for inviting us.

Cordially,

Incoming letter

Party for an Employee

Dear Jonathan,

On Thursday, January 11th, Mr. Mason will celebrate his 25th year with the Metropolitan organization. We who have worked with him for at least a part of this time have decided to recognize the occasion with a luncheon at the Hotel Sloane on that day, at 12:30 P.M. We're inviting some of the company's customers who know him well, and, of course, every member of his staff.

We'd be delighted if you can see your way clear to being with us. Will you drop me a line before January 4th, telling me if you can come? I certainly hope you can.

Cordially,

Answering letter

Dear Jack,

It will be a great pleasure to help Mr. Mason celebrate his 25th year at Metropolitan. You can count me in on the luncheon at the Hotel Sloane, January 11th, at 12:30 P.M.

Thanks very much.

Cordially,

Incoming letter

To Speak at Sales Luncheon

Dear Mr. Webster,

We heard your fascinating talk at the ANA luncheon last month and regretted that all of our salesmen weren't present to absorb your interesting point of view.

Your secretary tells me that you have a few open lunch dates on your agenda and that your usual fee for delivering your words of wisdom is $50. We'd like very much to have you address our 20-man sales staff on Wednesday, May 17th, at a luncheon meeting at the Atlas. The fee is an acceptable one and the food at the Atlas is pretty enticing, as you know. Is it possible for you to be with us? I'd appreciate a reply within the next week so that I may complete our plans for the meeting.

Cordially,

Answering letter

Dear Mr. Sturbridge,

I am very happy to accept your kind invitation to speak at the luncheon you are having for your sales staff on Wednesday, May 17th. When you have completed your plans, please let me know the time you would like me to be at the Atlas.

Cordially,

Incoming letter

A Reunion

Dear Miss Curtiss,

As an alumna of the Class of 1953, you'll be interested in knowing that the Vassar Grand Reunion is scheduled for the weekend starting with Friday, June 7th.

As you know, these Grand Reunions are held only every 25 years and alumnae throughout the country, throughout the world, in fact, attend in large numbers.

Since the Grand Reunion coincides with the tenth anniversary of your graduation from Vassar, the weekend should hold special meaning for you.

Attached is the agenda of planned events and a list of the dormitories and guest houses which can provide for visiting alumnae over that exciting weekend. If you wish to make reservations, all you need to do is fill in the attached postcard and accompany it with your check for $50, which will help to defray the costs of the Grand Reunion.

I hope that you can be with us.

Cordially,

Answering letter

Dear Miss Roddy,

I am looking forward with much pleasure to the Vassar Grand Reunion scheduled for the weekend starting Friday, June 7th.

My check for $50 is enclosed, along with the postcard on which I have filled in the required information.

Cordially,

Incoming letter

Reminder and Details on Convention

Dear Mr. Bennett,

Have you set aside the week of October 5th? We alerted you a few weeks ago so that you could plan to visit Miami and attend the Independent Merchants Convention there.

Now plans are specific. The seminars will be held at the Fontainebleu Hotel and sessions will start each morning at

9:30 A.M. in the Cort Room there. Lunch will be served either in the main dining room or at poolside from noon until 2:00 P.M. The rest of the afternoon is yours for fun and relaxation. Evening entertainment has been arranged and an interesting panel will amuse you during the dinner hour.

The cost of the entire week, including transportation by American Airlines from New York non-stop to Miami, is only $172. Charter planes will leave La Guardia Airport on the hour from 6:00 P.M. until midnight October 4th. To make your reservation, just fill in the blank spaces on the attached form and mail it back to me. No reservations can be accepted after September 10th.

You're in for a fabulous time, one that promises to be instructive and productive as well as entertaining. We'll see you in Miami, I hope.

Cordially,

Answering letter

Dear Mr. Sherwood,

Thank you for reminding me again of the Independent Merchants Convention to be held in Miami the week of October 5th. I had hoped until yesterday that it would be possible for me to attend, but now I find the rush of business here at the store makes it impossible.

However, I want our store to be represented, so I have asked my assistant buyer to take my place. I have filled out the form you sent me and am returning it with this letter.

Cordially,

Incoming letter

A Reception

Dear Mr. Carleton,

As President of the Legal Association of New York, it gives me pleasure to invite you to attend a reception honoring the Chief Justice of the Supreme Court of New York.

The reception will be held in the Central Memorial Coliseum at 1 Central Park West on Wednesday evening, January 21st. Cocktails will be served promptly at 7:30 P.M. to be followed by dinner at 8:00 P.M. It will be informal.

I sincerely hope you can attend. A reply will be appreciated.

Sincerely yours,

Answering letter

Dear Mr. Tabak,

Thank you very much for your kind invitation to attend the reception for the Chief Justice of the Supreme Court of New York.

I am very happy to say that I will be able to attend and that I am looking forward to meeting The Honorable Chief Justice, and to visiting with many of my old friends who will also be among the guests.

Cordially,

Incoming letter

Organizational Dinner—Guest Speaker

Dear Mr. Stuart,

I have been asked by the directors of the Manhattan Chapter of the North American Irish Association, to extend to you an invitation to be our guest speaker on March 17th at the St. Patrick's Day dinner to be held at the Lotos Club, 10 East 65th Street, at 6:30 P.M.

As you know, the N.A.I.A. is devoted to research in connection with Irish-American historical matters. As an expert in this field, we know your treatment of the subject will be extremely interesting to our members.

I'll send you further details a little later, but would so much like your acceptance as soon as possible, so that we may complete our agenda for that evening.

Cordially,

Answering letter

Dear Mr. Wigglesworth,

Thank you for asking me to be guest speaker at the St. Patrick's Day dinner to be held by the North American Irish Association at the Lotos Club.

I'm very sorry to report that I cannot accept your kind invitation because of a previous engagement. I would like to suggest, however, that my close associate John Henry O'Toole, who has been working with me for 15 years, and who has a vast knowledge of the subject you propose, might be an interesting speaker for your meeting. He will be here in my office during the coming week, if you would like to call him.

Cordially,

Incoming letter

A Business Luncheon—Prospective Employee

Dear Jim,

Are you free for lunch on Tuesday of next week (the 24th)? If you are, I'd like it so much if you can join Sam Merchant and me at about 12:30 at the Breevort.

Sam is the chap I mentioned to you on the telephone

the other day. He's an alert, up-and-coming salesman, and might just be the talent you're looking for. He'll be in town for only the one day.

Do let me know if you can make it.

Cordially,

Answering letter

Dear Ed,

I'm so glad that I'm free on Tuesday the 24th, for I'm most anxious to meet and talk to Sam. He may be just the man I'm looking for. I'll be at the Breevort at 12:30 sharp.

Thanks very much.

Cordially,

Incoming letter

A Club Banquet

Dear Mr. Whiting,

As a citizen with more than usual interest in foreign affairs, I think you'd enjoy hearing the speaker at the Press Club banquet on Thursday evening at the Hotel Pierre.

If this sounds attractive to you, won't you be my guest that evening? Cocktails will be served promptly at 7:00 with dinner around 7:30. The after-dinner speaker is Mort Tremblant, who may be known to you because of his recent book, *Our Overseas Affair.*

If you can join us, won't you let me know right away?

Cordially,

Answering letter

Dear Mr. Daniels,

It is very kind of you to want me as your guest at the Press Club banquet on Thursday evening at the Hotel Pierre.

It will be most interesting and informative to hear Mr. Tremblant. I've just finished reading *Our Overseas Affair*, and would like to see if he has anything to add about the events which have taken place since his book was printed.

I'll be at the Pierre at 7 o'clock and will look for you right away.

Cordially,

Incoming letter

A Drawing for a Prize

Dear Mr. Gentry,

For some months now, we've been experimenting with national advertising. This is something new for us and the results have been more than rewarding. It surprises us to see the range of inquiries from all parts of the world.

If you will read our August ad, you will note that we will have a drawing on May 27th next, offering a $5000 prize to the winner whose name will be drawn at random from the inquiries received during the month of August. This is, as you know, a device to attract more inquiries and greater attention to our products.

It would be very much appreciated if one of your "brass" would be good enough to attend the drawing and be a part of it. May we hear from you soon?

Cordially,

Answering letter

Dear Mr. Anderson,

We shall be more than happy to nâve Mr. Warner Bellows, the editor of Gentry's, attend the drawing on May 27th and be a part of it. Will you be sure to get in touch with Mr. Bellows some time previous to that date and instruct him where and when you will want him to appear and what you would like him to do?

Thanks so much for thinking of us. We are more than happy to participate.

Cordially,

XXI

Letters OF INTRODUCTION

When writing a letter of introduction, it should be remembered that the recipient is, in a sense, asked to perform a service or grant a favor. He may or may not be willing to cooperate and he should be permitted an opportunity to refrain if he chooses. Where possible, the letter should be mailed in advance of the arrival of the person it introduces. This gives the recipient a chance to refuse a meeting without the embarrassment of doing so in the presence of the party concerned.

The letter of introduction should include the name of the person being introduced, some personal or business data about him, and the reason for the introduction. Of course, it must also include a built-in alibi should the introduction be refused and a statement of sincere appreciation for the opportunity to make the introduction, if it is acceptable.

265

CHECK LIST

FOR LETTERS OF INTRODUCTION

1. Give name and background of person to be introduced.
2. Give reasons why recipient of letter may be pleased to meet him.
3. Give an "out" in case the introduction is not desired.
4. Thank recipient for cooperation, if it is possible.

Incoming letter

In Business

Dear Mr. Whitcomb,

May we introduce to you the Booth organization? We're new in Chicago, though we've been operating on a more local basis out of Detroit for 25 years. This expansion on our part now makes it possible for us to offer you the services of experienced public relation people—people whose experience is extremely diversified.

Our customers include the Whybe Company, Marvin Industries, and Madisonberger, all known to you, I am sure. Any one of these companies has assured me they'll be happy to answer your questions about us.

Meantime, I hope you'll read the enclosed brochure which outlines the services we can offer you.

I'll phone you on Thursday of next week with the hope that you can set aside a quarter of an hour sometime soon to discuss the ways in which Booth can help you to develop more business.

Cordially,

Answering letter

Dear Mr. Tryon,

Thank you for your letter about the Booth organization. After reading the brochure outlining the services you offer, I went over our own situation very carefully and decided that we are not in a position to make any changes in our system at this time. However, we may want to expand our advertising program next year—at which time I will surely ask you to send one of your representatives for further discussion.

Cordially,

Incoming letter

In Business

Dear Mr. Hagen,

I'd like to introduce to you Mrs. Mary Farnum, who is sort of a "housekeeper advisor" to us, helping us to plan from the homemaker's point of view our 1966 line of bed and bathroom linens.

Mrs. Farnum has some ideas in connection with linen services to the housewife which I think you will want to hear. They are unique in their concept, yet utterly feasible in their practicality. I think they can, once in effect, add to your profit picture during the forthcoming year.

Do drop me a line, after you've talked with Mrs. Farnum, to let me know your reaction.

Sincerely,

Answering letter

Dear Mr. Granby,

It just happened that I was out of town the week during which Mrs. Farnum called for an appointment. I would like very much to discuss with her any new ideas she has on linen services to the housewife. Will you please pass the word along to her to phone me again next week for an appointment? Thanks so much for putting us in touch with her, Mr. Hagen.

Cordially,

Incoming letter

In Business

Dear Dave,

Rob Manion, bearer of this letter, was my roommate at Princeton and though, just on that score alone, I'd like you to know him, there's an even more important reason. Rob was recently appointed territorial manager in charge of field operations for H. B. Smith & Company. In other words, he's doing the same kind of work in the Southwest that you are doing up North. He surprised me by telling me you didn't know each other, but I suppose that shouldn't be so much of a surprise with a company whose tentacles are as widespread as Smith's.

However, it struck me that you and Rob might have a lot in common and enjoy not only knowing each other, but have fun comparing notes, so I've told him to pass this letter in to you via your secretary. Rob understands how busy you are, so please don't feel obligated to see him unless it's both convenient and sounds interesting. If you do get together, I'm sure you both will enjoy the experience.

Sincerely,

Answering letter

Dear Rich,

It was a great pleasure to meet Rob Manion. He stopped in last week and we went out for lunch at the *Brown Derby*. We had a fine visit, and a good discussion of the work we are both doing in the same field. We've made plans to keep in touch.

Thanks for being so thoughtful in bringing us together.

Cordially,

Incoming letter

A Friendly Gesture

Dear Vincent,

My very good friend Fred Erbe will be visiting Omaha sometime early next week. I took the liberty of telling him to look in on you.

Fred is in charge of advertising for one of the big ad agencies, Maynard and Stone, out here and I think you two would have a lot in common. This is his first trip to Omaha and I'd appreciate any courtesy you may care to extend to him. On the other hand, both of us will understand if your time is pre-empted by matters which arose long before you ever received this letter. My very best to Sue.

Sincerely,

Answering letter

Dear Culver,

Fred called me right after he arrived here in Omaha last week and I invited him out to the house for dinner last evening. We had a grand time visiting and found that we had so much in common that we are looking forward to a continued friendship.

Thanks a lot for sharing Fred with us.

Cordially,

Incoming letter

A Bank's Reference

Dear Mr. McCurdy,

On February 23rd, I shall leave for Europe aboard the Queen Mary, arriving in Southampton on February 28th. The purpose of my trip is to interest foreign manufacturers in the sale of their products in the United States.

Since it is doubtful my firm will be known to most of the people I hope to see, I think a letter of introduction to the leading bank in each of the following cities might prove very helpful to me: Antwerp, Geneva, Rome, Paris and London.

Because I and my company are known to you over a period of many years, I wonder, Mr. McCurdy, if you could give me such letters of introduction? The favor would be very much appreciated, indeed.

Cordially,

Answering letter

To Whom It May Concern,

This letter is to introduce Mr. Joseph Collerd, who represents the firm of Everlasting Perfumes, Inc., of 289 Madison Avenue, New York City, New York.

We have known Mr. Collerd for the past 15 years, and can say with assurance that he is a gentleman of fine character and personality. The firm he represents is and has always been in good standing with our offices here in New York City.

Any favors you may see fit to grant Mr. Collerd, as a representative of Everlasting Perfumes, will be much appreciated.

Cordially,

Incoming letter

For Job Hunting

Dear Mr. Sentinel,

When we lunched together last month, I mentioned John Merck as a possible candidate for the accounting job you said would open up soon. Since then, I've talked to John and he is very much interested in knowing more about the requirements.

This, then, will introduce him to you. His background with Mansfield and Company has given him excellent training, and his extremely pleasant personality and fine character should make him well worth your consideration.

I most certainly appreciate your courtesy in seeing him.

Cordially,

Answering letter

Dear Mr. Wyatt,

Thank you for sending John Merck in to see me. We've had a nice chat and I've asked him to fill in a couple of our usual forms, just because that's our policy.

I think we have something for John and he has something for us. It's my hope we can fit him into the picture here, and soon.

Cordially,

Incoming letter

In Research

Dear Mr. Gibbs,

This letter will introduce a former associate of mine, Mr. Thomas Robinson, who is now secretary to the Engineering Society.

The Society which Mr. Robinson represents is making a thorough study of the frequency modulation situation, as it concerns the number of FM stations operating on the band at the present time.

I've told him of your interest in the subject of FM and of the fact that you were the first manufacturer to come out with a consumer version of the FM tuner. He'd like very much to talk to you about all of this, with the hope that you'll give him some of your ideas about the problems that exist.

I shall surely appreciate it if you have a little time to talk with Mr. Robinson.

Cordially,

Answering letter

Dear Mr. Swanson,

Thank you very much for letting me know about Thomas Robinson. I've heard a great deal about his work in the research field, and was most anxious to meet him.

I hadn't much time when he stopped in, but we've made an appointment for next Thursday morning.

Cordially,

XXII

Internal LETTERS OR MEMOS

꽃 Written communication in business is often just as important internally (within the office, the division, the corporation and its branch offices) as it is externally. While much interoffice communication can be verbal, wherever specific facts or figures are used it's more reliable to put them in writing. This makes future reference simple; it leaves no doubt as to what is meant; it makes a more definitive impact; it leaves very little room for error.

Nearly all the rules which apply to external communication are essential to the internal variety, too, though often (not always) a more informal approach may be taken.

CHECK LIST
FOR INTERNAL LETTERS OR MEMOS

1. Be just as polite as if you were dealing with a client.

2. Be clear and graphic.
3. Give opportunity for further discussion, if necessary.
4. Thank the recipient for his anticipated cooperation.
5. Throw in a word of praise, if possible.

Incoming letter

Rewarding Salesmen

TO THE SALESMEN OF EUROPA COMPANY

When I attended your last sales meeting in New York, I came away feeling, as president of this company, that our sales activities couldn't be in better hands. Primarily, I was excited about your *enthusiasm!*

I have always felt that there is no more important qualification for a salesman. If he isn't enthusiastic about his job, his company, the products he offers, he just can't sell with sincerity.

My enthusiasm about *your* enthusiasm caused me to spend a lot of time in the past few weeks figuring out how we can continue to keep you enthusiastic. We shall always put out products of which you are proud, of course. We shall continue to offer you and the customers you serve the benefit of our manufacturing skill. We shall keep ourselves aware of industrial changes and improvements.

But I can think of nothing more rewarding to you than to become a part owner of the Europa Company. And this is now possible.

Effective on Monday, January 3rd, every salesman will receive from me without charge one share of Europa common stock. Current market value at the time of this writing is approximately $110 and the last quarterly dividend was $5.60. At the same time, there will be made available to you, under a new and specially-designed by-law, as many shares of Europa as you wish to purchase for a full 10 percent less than the

market value of the stock on the day you make your purchase. This offer is open to you until January 31st, 1965.

If you think you were enthusiastic about Europa before
this, just wait until you're a stockholder. And you're building
a financial future for yourself right within the walls of the
very company which pays you your salary! How can you
help being even more enthusiastic?

I hope you'll be pleased as I am at this opportunity. If
you have any questions, just let me know.

Cordially,

Answering letter

Dear Mr. McGinnis,

I want to thank you for the share of Europa common
stock which I received in the mail this morning. I certainly
hope to take advantage of the offer to purchase more stock at
10 percent less than the market value, just as soon as I pay
off a few bills that are presently outstanding.

May I add that I believe this gesture on your part will
induce the salesmen to work harder than ever toward the
greater success of Europa. . . .

Cordially,

Incoming letter

Welcome to a New Employee

TO: Mr. John Doe

I'm so happy to welcome you to the Mason and Merrit
Company. I think one of the first things you'll notice is the
extreme loyalty and interest expressed by practically every

one of our workers, whether in the offices or in the manufacturing plant.

One of the reasons for this is, Mr. Doe, that we think of our employees as *people*—human beings who have personal lives and problems outside of the realm of their activities with us.

You'll find that each department head is more than willing to discuss your problems with you, whether they have to do with your job or the need for some sort of assistance in your personal life.

We try to protect our employees as far as possible in connection with accident and life insurance, hospitalization and ample vacation periods. Additional fringe benefits in the form of a pension and profit-sharing plan are also available after you are with us a full 90 days.

Please feel free to ask any questions that occur to you. Meantime, I'm very pleased to know that you have joined our family.

Cordially,

Answering letter

Dear Mr. Peabody,

Your very thoughtful letter of welcome was on my desk when I arrived this morning. I feel it a privilege to be a part of Mason and Merrit and can assure you I will do my utmost to contribute more and more to its future success.

Thank you very much.

Cordially,

Incoming letter

Dear Mr. Goldmeyer,

For the last two weeks the salesmen coming in from the surrounding territory have reported to me a rumor going around that we are going out of business. I don't believe this is true, of course. But obviously something is going on and I hope you'll let us know very soon what it is so that we can refute the ugly rumors.

Cordially,

Answering letter

Clarifying a Rumor

Dear Staff Members,

I'm sure that nearly all of you have heard rumors of one sort or another in the past few months to the effect that the company for which you work is "going out of business," "being sold," or "merged."

The latter rumor happens to be more than a rumor—it's a fact. Effective January 1st, we will become a wholly-owned subsidiary of The Acton Company of Minneapolis.

Principals at The Acton Company have asked me to let you know that it is their intention to continue to operate this division on an autonomous basis and to retain all employees who are presently on our payroll.

There are many benefits to be gained from this merger, some of which will affect you personally. Mr. Harry Acton, president of the organization, will be here on Monday, January 4th, to talk with you and give you some idea of future plans.

I'm sure you'll approve this merger wholeheartedly once you understand its many advantages to both employer and employees.

Very truly yours,

Incoming letter

Requesting Cooperation

TO: ALL CLERICAL EMPLOYEES

Attached is a brochure outlining in detail the uses to which we will put our recently-acquired computer.

This new machine will make it possible for us to issue detailed reports on a variety of our operations. We have always needed such reports, but because they had to be done manually, we have frequently neglected to issue them in the past.

At first, many of you will probably find computerized reports strange and a little difficult to understand. Once you absorb the coding principal outlined in the brochure, you'll begin to recognize the benefits to be enjoyed by each department.

Converting to computer will take a little time at first and I ask your patience until we have completed this gigantic task.

I'll be happy to have Mr. Johnson take you through our accounting and statistical department, if you'd like an advance idea of what the computer will eventually do for us.

Very truly yours,

Answering letter

Dear Mr. Wilson,

In addition to reading the brochure—which I must admit has me a little puzzled—I need to see the computer in action, to clear up some questions in my mind. I'll stop by on Thursday, at 10:30 A.M. for a tour with Mr. Johnson, if that time meets with his and your approval.

Cordially,

Incoming letter

Preventative Medicine

TO: ALL EMPLOYEES

We're very pleased to announce that we are now able to offer each and every one of our employees a complete physical examination without charge.

Now I'm sure many of you will say: "So what?", but I hope I can nevertheless induce you to take advantage of this opportunity.

The progress of medicine today has made it possible to prevent many, many illnesses if precautions are taken in time. Also possible in this fast-striding twentieth century is the early prediction of what ailments may develop through environmental or hereditary studies.

A thorough physical examination like the one we're now able to offer would cost a minimum of $75 if you had it done privately. Now you can check up on your health--without spending a single nickel of your own.

Appointments are now being made with department heads for these physical examinations. I hope we'll have 100 percent of our employees taking advantage of this worthwhile opportunity.

Very truly yours,

Answering letter

Dear Miss Hansen,

In response to the letter from Mr. Jones about physical examinations for all the employees, I would like to make an appointment for Friday morning at 10 o'clock. If this is not convenient will you let me know right away, please?

Cordially,

Incoming letter

A Sales Meeting

TO: ALL SALESMEN

There will be a national sales meeting at the Hotel Plaza starting at 9:00 A.M. Wednesday, September 10th, and running through Friday, September 12th at 5:00 P.M.

A complete agenda will be mailed to you shortly, but meantime you may want to make arrangements for both transportation and overnight accommodations as soon as possible.

If you wish to stay at the Hotel Plaza, write my secretary at once, since we have a special arrangement there which will entitle you to a group discount for your room.

All salesmen are expected to attend this meeting and if there are reasons why this may prove difficult, I'd appreciate a written note from you right away.

Cordially,

Answering letter

Dear Miss Ancheks,

In response to the letter I received this morning from Mr. Cary, please reserve a single room and bath for me at the Hotel Plaza, where I understand we will get a discount.

I will want these accommodations for the three days of the meeting—which means that I will arrive at the Plaza on Tuesday afternoon about 4:00 P.M.

Thank you very much.

Cordially,

Incoming letter

Watching Expenses

TO: OUR EMPLOYEES

The economic indicators, in the main, are pointing 1965 sales graphs up . . . up . . . and *up!* And our own sales projections show that we are in agreement with the majority. Business is good now, but all signs seem to point toward even greater sales revenue as the year progresses.

To this optimistic note, I must, however, attach a word of warning. Higher sales and sales revenue are not very valuable and cannot lead to higher profits unless the expense budget is watched most carefully. Can it profit a company to increase its annual sales income by, let's say, 20 percent, if its expenses increase by 20 percent or more?

Let's keep an eagle eye on our expenses this year. Let's eliminate every possible penny of waste expense. Let's make every expense dollar count. If all of us join hands in this area, I can safely predict that higher sales in 1965 can mean bigger bonuses at the year's end for each and every employee.

Will each of you send me a memo soon telling me what steps you are taking to cut expenses?

Sincerely,

Answering letter

Dear Mr. Goldberg,

I will do my best to cut 1965 expenses wherever possible but, as you know, we are operating at just about a minimum even now. The only area where some savings might be accomplished is if you're willing to put our three day men on a Saturday shift and pay them time and a half, thereby eliminating the night shift entirely. Can we discuss this sometime soon, please?

Cordially,

Appendix FORMS OF ADDRESS

ADDRESSEE	SALUTATION	ENVELOPE
	Nobility	
Baron	My Lord or Dear Sir	Lord _____ full name
Baroness	My Lady or Dear Madame	Lady _____ full name
Duchess	Madame or Dear Duchess	Her Grace, the Duchess of _____
Duke	Sir or Dear Duke	His Grace, the Duke of _____
Earl	My Lord	The Right Honorable the Earl of _____

ADDRESSEE	SALUTATION	ENVELOPE
King	May it please Your Majesty	His Majesty, King _____
Knight	Sir	Sir _____ full name

Office—Appointive

ADDRESSEE	SALUTATION	ENVELOPE
Ambassador (U.S.)	Sir or My dear Mr. Ambassador	The Honorable _____ full name
Ambassador (foreign)	Sir or My dear Mr. Ambassador	His Excellency, Ambassador of _____ full name
Cabinet Officer (U.S.)	Sir (or Madame) or My dear Mr. (or Madame) Secretary	The Honorable _____ full name
Chief Justice of Supreme Court or Associate Justice	Sir or My dear Mr. Chief Justice or Mr. Justice	The Honorable _____ full name

Office—Elective

ADDRESSEE	SALUTATION	ENVELOPE
Congressman	Sir or My dear Representative	The Honorable _____
Governor	Sir or My dear Governor	The Honorable _____
Mayor	Sir or My dear Mr. Mayor	The Honorable _____

ADDRESSEE	SALUTATION	ENVELOPE
President of the U.S.	Sir or My dear Mr. President	The President
Senator	Sir or My dear Senator	The Honorable _____
Vice-President of U.S.	Sir or My dear Mr. Vice-President	The Vice-President

Religious

ADDRESSEE	SALUTATION	ENVELOPE
Archbishop	Your Excellency or Most Reverend Sir	The Most Reverend _____ full name
Bishop	Dear Bishop _____ surname or Your Excellency	The Right Reverend _____ full name or The Most Reverend _____ full name
Cardinal	Your Eminence	His Eminence, Cardinal _____ full name
Minister	My Dear Mr. _____ surname or My Dear Dr. _____ surname	The Reverend _____ full name
Monsignor	Right Reverend Monsignor	The Right Reverend Monsignor _____ full name

ADDRESSEE	SALUTATION	ENVELOPE
Nun	My dear Sister or Dear Sister _____ surname	Sister _____ surname
Priest	Reverend Sir or My dear Father _____ surname	The Reverend _____ full name
Rabbi	My dear Rabbi or My dear Dr. _____ surname	Rabbi _____ full name

Index

Index

A

Accidents, letters of sympathy following, 136–138

Accountants, letters of recommendation, 120

Achievement, letters of congratulations, 65–67

Acknowledgment, letters of, 11–16
appointments, 14–15
changes in order, 15
check list for, 11
for forgotten articles, 16
receipt of book, 12–13
request for information, 13–14
speaking engagements, 12

Address, change of, 243–245

Address, forms of, 283–286
addressee, 283–286
envelope, 283–286
nobility, 283–284
salutation, 283–286

Adjustments, letters requesting, 39–41

Advertising:
announcements, 247–248
drawing for prizes, 262–263
letters of appreciation, 90–91
in new publication, 250–251
sales letters, 143–144, 162–163
soliciting, 186–187
use of coupons, 162–163

Agreements, confirmation of verbal, 3–4, 45

Airlines:
reservations, 128–129
routing trip, 128–129

Ambassadors, forms of address, 284

Announcement, letters of, 241–251
advertising in new publication, 250–251
advertising rate increase, 247–248
check list for, 241
mergers, 249
new location, 243–245
new salesman, 248–249
new stockholders, 246–247
new telephone number, 245–246
retirement, 242
sales meetings, 279–280

Apology, letters of, 29–43
adjustment, 39–40
admitting error of omission, 37–38
check list, 30
delay caused by illness, 35–36
due to illness, 30–31
employer out of town, 32–33, 35–36
equipment out of order, 37
forgotten luncheon date, 41–42
general delay, 31–32, 33–34
letters requesting adjustments, 39–41
referring request to another, 30–31, 34–35
suggesting another use for delayed goods, 42–43
unavoidable change of schedule, 38–39

Appointments:
acknowledging, 14–15
authority to make, 25
cancelling, 20–22
because of illness, 21–23
employer out of town, 20–21
change of dates for, 53
changes made by secretary, 2–3
confirmation, 53
delayed action letters, 24–25

O

Options, requests for extension, 190–191, 200

Orders:
acknowledging changes in, 15
billed for goods not ordered, 77–78
lack of, 147–148
quantity buying, 184–188
requesting future, 173–174

P

Packaging methods, sales letters, 158–159
Pamphlets, sales letters offering, 153–154
Payment methods:
confirmation of, 55–56
letters of complaint about, 82–84
offer of, 236–237
sales letters on, 159–160
Payment overdue, reminder of, 229–230, 232–234
Periodicals, requesting renewal, 188–189
Personal achievement, letters of congratulations, 65–67
Personal secretary, letters of recommendation, 112–114
Persuasion, letters of, 183–193
alleviating fear, 185–186
check list for, 184
to clarify misunderstanding, 189–190
giving additional information, 191–192
option on real estate, 190–191
purpose of, 183–184
for quantity buying, 184–185
soliciting advertising, 186–187
subscription renewal, 188–189
use of statistical information, 192–193
Political candidates:
letters of congratulations, 60–61
refusal to back, 224–225
Political news column, letters of appreciation, 99–100
President of United States, forms of address, 285
Price, letters of complaint, 84–85
Priests, forms of address, 286
Products, sales letters stressing improvements, 158
Promotions, letters of congratulation, 61–62
Public relations, good will letters, 165–182

R

Rabbis, forms of address, 286
Real estate:
confirming time of closing, 54
option on, 190–191, 200
Receptions, invitations to, 258–259
Recommendation, letters of, 111–122
accountants, 120
check list, 112
open letter of, 115–116
personal secretary, 112–114
sales manager with physical handicap, 118
salesmen with physical handicaps, 117–118
secretarial or clerical position, 114–115
service industry, 121
of slightly known person, 111
statistical position, 115–116
travel promotion, 119
Reference, letters of, 111 (*See also* Recommendation, letters of)
bank's reference, 269–270
open letter of, 115–116
Refusal, letters of, 217–225
to attend meeting, 219–221
to back political candidate, 224–225
care in planning, 217
check list for, 217–218
contributions, 218–219
interviews, 221–223
proffered honor, 223–224
Religious dignitaries, forms of address, 285–286
Reminder letters, 103–109
to attend convention, 257–258
attendance at seminar, 108–109
business luncheons, 104
check list, 103–104
on conducting a seminar, 107–108
date of meeting, 109
about new merchandise, 104–105
purpose of, 103
on sales promotions, 105–107
Reports, letters of appreciation for, 91–92
Request, letters of, 195–216
for additional information, 199–200, 210–211
for appointments, 195, 205–207
check list for, 195–196
for completion of lists, 197
confirming enrollment of student, 214–215